A History of the Cameroon

Tambi Eyongetah
B.A. *(Soc.)* *(Nsukka)*, M.Sc. *(Soc.Sc.)* *(Edin)*
and
Robert Brain
(formerly lecturer in anthropology at University College, London)

LONGMAN

**Longman
1724 - 1974**

Longman Group Limited
London

Associated companies, branches and
representatives throughout the world

© Longman Group Ltd 1974

First published 1974

ISBN 0 582 60254 8

*Filmset in Hong Kong by
Asco Trade Typesetting Ltd and
printed in Hong Kong by
Dai Nippon Printing Co (HK) Ltd*

Dedicated to, and in memory of
my late father, Samuel Eyongetah.

Acknowledgements

The publishers are grateful to the following for permission to reproduce photographs:

Agence Hoa-Qui: pp. 18, 31, 37, 43, 45 and cover photograph; Archiv fur Kunst und Gescgichte: p. 67; Cameroon Information Service: pp. 131, 132, 140, 168 and 115; Tabi Egbe: p. 172; J.N. Foncha: p. 139; Her Majesty's Stationary Office (with the permission of the Controller of Her Majesty's Stationary Office): p. 110; Historisches Bildarchiv: p. 80; S.T. Muna: p. 171; Radio Times Hulton Picture Library: p. 28.

List of Maps

		page
1	Physical features and bordering countries	2
2	Tribal allocation in Anglophone Cameroon	7
3	Old trade routes across the Eastern Sahara and Hanno's route to Mount Cameroon	10
4	Four major language divisions	20
5	The Central Cameroon Highlands	35
6	Zintgraff's journey	69
7	German concessions	82
8	The sub-division of British Cameroon	96
9	Major towns and communications	102
10	Plantations in west Cameroon	105
11	Cameroon immediately post re-unification	161
12	The two western provinces after the 1972 changes in Cameroon	176

Contents

PREFACE   vi
CHAPTER   1   Geography and peoples   1
           2   Mount Cameroon and the 'discovery' of   9
                Cameroon
           3   Cameroon and the Sudan   12
           4   The Sao civilisation   17
           5   The peopling of the Cameroon   19
           6   Islam and the North   27
           7   The Central Cameroon Highlands   34
           8   The coastal peoples   50
           9   European traders and the Coast   53
          10   The scramble for the Cameroon   58
          11   The Germans explore in Cameroon   65
          12   Wars against the Germans   72
          13   Missionaries in the Cameroon   76
          14   Land and labour under the Germans   79
          15   German administration   90
          16   British Cameroons   95
          17   British and French rule compared   113
          18   Early political developments   119
          19   Cameroonian nationalism in the Southern
                Cameroons   128
          20   Reunification   146
          21   The Federal Constitution   159
          22   Post-Reunification politics in Cameroon   167
BIBLIOGRAPHY   182

Preface

This book is by two authors, one an anthropologist who has worked on the traditional history of the various peoples of Cameroon, the other an historian who is concerned with a detailed appraisal of the development of self-government in western Cameroon, the former British Cameroons, and the progress towards reunification. By our co-operation we have tried to avoid traditional biases in histories of developing states whereby either complex tribal studies swamp contemporary history, or detailed constitutional processes since colonial times provide the bulk of the 'history' of the state.

In a book of this kind the authors have to depend on secondary sources as much as primary sources and we should like to express our gratitude to scholars such as Dr. Phyllis Kaberry, Mrs Sally Chilver and Edwin Ardener, D. Gardinier, V.T. Le Vine and Neville Rubin whose contributions to the study of political and traditional institutions have been of such great help. Mention should also be made of *Germans in the Cameroons, 1884–1919* by the late H. Rudin, which has been invaluable as source material to both authors. We particularly wish to mention these authors since our policy has been not to encumber the work with references and footnotes, so that their influence is not immediately apparent in the text itself.

Cameroonian history, at least before the twentieth century, is not difficult to write in so far as the sources for the early periods are few and far between. One 'written' document for the Cameroon concerns the discovery by the Carthaginian Hanno of Mount Cameroon. After that, unfortunately, we have a gap of over a thousand years and it is during this period that many of the most important questions relevant to the peopling of Cameroon have to be solved. These include such subjects as the origin of the Bantu peoples, the motive behind their migrations and the relationship of the Cameroon peoples to this wider grouping of people. We shall seek our answers in the study of language distribution and cultural innovations such as iron-working and new

food crops. Then we shall look more closely at certain tribal movements and political developments, using oral traditions and some
written documents to present a general picture of the ethnic ('tribal'
as it used to be called) situation in the Cameroons as it was at the time
of the penetration of Europeans beyond the coastal regions into the
interior at the end of the nineteenth century. Before the more complete account of Cameroon constitutional history and contemporary
developments in the twentieth century, we shall also approach the
later history of Cameroon for which we have limited written records,
the Fulani migrations, the northern lamidats, European traders of the
coast and the early colonial period (under the Germans, and then as
mandated territories under the British and French).

In this introductory history, written in English, for English-
speaking Cameroonians, more space is given to Anglophone western
Cameroon than to the larger eastern Cameroon. The reason for this
is that French-speaking Cameroon has been amply served by its historians, particularly Mveng whose *Histoire du Cameroun* is a standard text,
although Mveng and other French-speaking historians have ignored
the history of the fomer West Cameroon. Western Cameroon also
deserves a history of its own, because it has its own separate character
and, in some ways, forms a cultural unit separate from eastern
Cameroon. This is not only because of its colonial associations with
Great Britain and the artificial boundaries which originally divided
the French and British Trust Territories after the defeat of Germany
in the first world war. The southern mountain range (Manenguba
and Bambuti) has served to cut off the west from the east to a certain
extent, although in the north there are fewer natural barriers between
the two federated states – the Bamenda and Bamileke Grassfields, for
example, are really one.

Nevertheless, some indications of historical developments in the
east are vital to an understanding of western Cameroon's past as well
as its present, since events and movements of peoples in the east and
north have affected the whole of the Cameroon. A spate of raids and
whole-scale invasions by the Fulani of the nineteenth century had
repercussions in the Grassfields and were even felt as far south as the
forest lands of eastern Cameroon. It is this general involvement of the
whole country in movements of peoples and cultural transformations
that we try to bring out in this introduction to Cameroon history.
Rather than recording a detailed examination of isolated 'tribes' or
single events we shall trace connections between events, establish
trends and see Cameroon history as part of the history of this African
region as a whole.

Geography and peoples

The history of Cameroon before 1914 is not difficult to write. This is due only to the paucity of material available at the present time and not to the straightforwardness and simple themes of this country's history. Hemmed in between Chad, Gabon and Nigeria, it is a small country of just over five million inhabitants, speaking different languages, living in diverse cultural and environmental niches.

Let us look at the geography first. Cameroon is a country of fairly distinct regions: mangrove swamps, coastal plains, a central plateau, the great Chad plains in the north, heavily wooded lowlands to the south-east and an important range of mountains which begins in the south with Mount Cameroon and stretches north to Adamawa (see map on p. 2). Like most West African states Cameroon is divided into belts determined by climate and vegetation from the humid forest region along the coast, which may be drenched in a hundred inches (25400 mm) of rain over eight or nine months of the year (Debundscha in Fako with almost for hundred inches (101600 mm) a year has the second highest rainfall in the world), to the desert margins nearly a thousand miles (1609 km) away in the north. These zones link Cameroon geographically with neighbouring countries. There are few natural boundaries dividing Cameroon from its neighbours and this factor is of considerable importance in tracing Cameroon's past. To some degree present-day cultural and linguistic differences are marked by these geographical zones and that is why we can talk with some truth of 'Grassfields' people, the 'coastal' Bantu, the peoples of the south-east forests, the 'savannah' people.

The geographical zones which cross state frontiers link Cameroon peoples with other nationals. The stretch of savannah and orchard bush in the north extends from North Cameroon beyond Lake Chad into Northern Nigeria and the Sudan. The coastal mangrove swamps of the south extend into the delta of the Niger in south-east Nigeria and the coastal equatorial forest of eastern Cameroon continues in

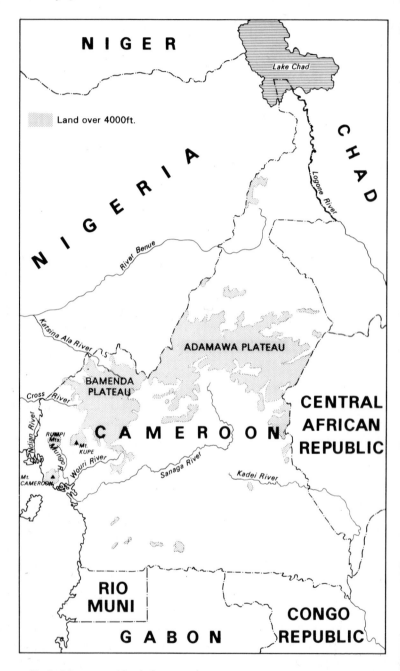

1 Physical features and bordering countries

Gabon. In the centre the highland plateau crosses the whole of Cameroon and links it with similar regions and related peoples in north-eastern Nigeria. Since the history of the Cameroon is bound up with the characteristics of these regions we shall discuss them in a little more detail before embarking on a strictly historical – that is chronological – account.

Mountains

Mountains are everywhere a limiting factor in the history of settlement and migration. On the whole Cameroon is a hilly and mountainous country, the reasons for this dating back some 300 million years. It is generally accepted that from this period onwards South America became separated from western Africa to which it was originally attached, a process which lasted many million years. As a result of this drifting apart of continents a 'fault line' (a series of weaknesses in the structure of the earth's surface) appeared in the northern part of Africa.

The new shape of the continent led to a period of mountain building which adjusted the balance of the earth's surface in West Africa. Most of this mountain building occurred in the Cameroon and was followed by a period of intense volcanic activity. The most typical volcanic region is the Bamenda Highlands, an area almost entirely overlaid by volcanic stone.

Apart from Bamenda we find further south a number of volcanic structures: Kupe, Manenguba, Rumpi and Mount Cameroon as well as the Atlantic islands of Fernando Po, Principe and Sao Thomé, which are part of the same volcanic activity. The chain of single volcanoes finds its peak on the Cameroon coast in Mount Cameroon which at over 12,000 feet (4,000 m) is West Africa's highest mountain and a still active volcano. Low-lying regions in the Cameroon have formed draining channels of watersheds for these mountains, such as the Mamfe Cross River depression and the Douala and Tiko Plains.

Cameroon has no specifically mountain peoples, although many groups and communities have lived in mountain areas or sought refuge in hilly country from the attacks of slave-raiders or the infiltrations of new immigrants. The Bakweri, for example, lived high in the foothills of Mount Cameroon; the Bangwa have adapted to mountain regions up to 6,000 feet (2,000 m) high; while the Kapsiki in North Cameroon built stone villages in the hills to shelter from the raids of Fulani mounted warriors.

3

The central highlands

The volcanic mountain groups of central Cameroon merge into a high plateau (Bamenda in western Cameroon) which is over 3,000 feet (1,000 m) high on the whole, with much higher individual peaks. In this region there are also a number of alluvial plains which are good farming areas – the Ndop and the Mbaw plains are the most important. The Bamenda plateau is also continuous with a similar region in eastern Cameroon which is usually known as the Bamileke Grassfields. This whole central zone is a smooth, open area which offers ease of movements to both invaders and wandering peoples; the Grassfields as a result have been subject to countless shifts in population and changes in social structure. There are large kingdoms (Nsaw and Bamum), small city states (Bali, Bafut) and autonomous villages (Meta, Ngie). This central plateau merges into the Adamawa plateau to the north and it continues north-east into eastern Cameroon, gradually levelling off towards the Lake Chad drainage basin. Here live the so-called Tikar groups – Banyo and Margi as well as Kapsiki, Fulani, Hausa, 'Arabs'.

The coastal plains and hills

The lowland plains of Cameroon are found inland from the 220 mile (354 km) coastline. These equatorial forests spread out in a fan towards the east, reaching as far as tributaries of the Congo in the south-east. In western Cameroon this forest zone stops in the vicinity of Kumba and Tombel. In the east the coastal plain continues as far as the Douala basin. Here the average height above sea level is barely 100 feet (30 m). Due to the enormous rainfall there are also coastal mangrove swamps; the western mangroves are cut up delta-wise by the innumerable tributaries of the Ndian and Lekele rivers which rise from the Oban-Rumpi range.

In this region we find important Bantu peoples: the Maka, Djem and Douala, the Fang and Beti, the Bakweri, Bakundu, Bakossi, Basossi and the Mbo. These peoples are the most northern section of the vast grouping of Bantu-speaking peoples which stretches from Cameroon to East and South Africa. Migrations out of and into this coastal plain, in the recent past, have altered any overall simple pattern that may have existed. There are also Efik fishermen, non-Bantu groups from Nigeria, living in the mangrove areas such as the 'Fish Towns' of the Rio del Rey.

The coast

Fako Division, dominated by the volcanic Cameroon Mountain (13,350 feet) [4069 m] has a high rainfall and fertile soils. It is separated from the neighbouring coastal regions of Calabar as well as Douala by the Rio del Rey and Wouri estuaries and mangrove swamps. Here we have the large banana and cocoa plantations, originally established by the Germans. The ports are Victoria and Tiko. 'Old Cameroons' is the coastal stretch between Douala and Victoria, the main commercial and government centre of Kamerun. The regions were linked by water transport and some interchange of population. While the territory was divided in 1922 with the mandate settlement and the ports became more and more isolated from each other, in the next thirty years a sense of contact remained, fortified by the use of Pidjin English.

The mountain slopes of Fako Division were the site of a large plantation industry established by the Germans after 1885. These estates were maintained in operation up to the second world war, primarily under their original owners. In 1940 they fell to the government and in 1947 the estates were sequestered and leased to a public body, the Cameroon Development Corporation (CDC), whose profits (under the term of its charter) were to go to the Trust Territory. These CDC estates still remain the chief industrial resource of present-day western Cameroon.

In Cameroon the Mamfe depression is a region apart. This is the home of the Cross River which links west Cameroon with south-east Nigeria. To the south, west and north of this hilly land there is a semi-circular range of mountains and the depression is a receiving area for the innumerable streams which issue from this mountain range. Here we have a low-lying fertile land, although hot swampy conditions sometimes make cultivation difficult. There are huge forest reserves such as Kembong, Mbo, Takamanda. Peoples include the Banyang, one of a group of related peoples inhabiting the largest part of Manyu Division. Within the division itself this group includes, besides the Banyang, their northern neighbours living on the 'overside' of the Cross River, generally referred to as Anyang, and also a section of the Keyaka-Ekoi peoples (Obang, Ekwe, Keaka) who live to the west of the Banyang and are widely distributed in neighbouring Nigeria. They are also linked through language relationship and historical traditions to similar peoples (Ibibio, Mbembe) in south-east Nigeria. Among the Banyang a distinction is made between Upper and Lower Banyang, the Upper Banyang being those who live in the eastern part of the country towards the source of the tributary rivers which flow through it, and the Lower Banyang inhabiting its western part in which the rivers converge to form the mainstream of the Cross River.

'Tribes'

In discussing groupings of people such as the Bantu, semi-Bantu, the Bamenda peoples, the Bamileke, the North-West Bantu, we come up against a problem inherent in the use of the word 'tribe' in Africa and, particularly in the Cameroon where small states, linguistic groups, a haphazard collection of villages banded together by a European district officer were called 'tribes'. In this book, while admittedly trying to draw a sort of 'tribal map' of Cameroon, we are very conscious that the boundaries between groups of peoples, tribes, ethnic groups are very vague. Colonial administrators, of course, liked these boundaries to be as precise as possible and their attempts at making neat and classified tribal lists often led to confusion: 'Widekum', 'Keyaka', 'Tikari' are all examples of terms used by Europeans for political or linguistic units or only vaguely connected groups which were never really clearly marked off as separate ethnic groups.

In Fako Division and Meme Division all the peoples (except the Korup and the Efik) speak Bantu languages of the North-Western group. In the central and north of west Cameroon there are many other languages which Europeans have labelled as Bantoid (a group related to each other and also to Bantu). The language frontier crosses the former inter-state boundaries from west to east and Bantoid languages of the Cross River type are cut from north to south by the Nigerian boundary. It would be a mistake to imagine, however, that linguistic connections imply any degree of 'tribalism'; they merely speak the same language in the same way that the French and Italians can be said to speak the same language.

Environment and social organisation play an important part in setting people off from each other, as much as language does. Within the forest region of the Cameroon, for example, there are important differences between people looking towards the Cross River for their social and economic contacts (particularly in Manyu and their relationship with south-east Nigeria), and the peoples who look towards the coast (peoples of Meme and Fako). Other peoples are distinguished, not through language or economic systems, but in that they enjoy traditional political systems of a state type with chiefs, queen mothers, servant classes, like the chiefdoms of Bamenda, or simpler, more egalitarian village organisations of such peoples as the Banyang and Mbo.

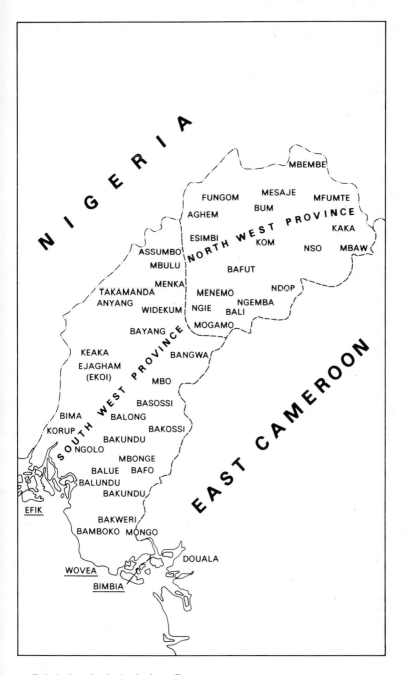

2 Tribal allocation in Anglophone Cameroon

These cultural, linguistic and geographical boundaries make any clear definition of cultural areas very different; and words like 'tribe' have to be used with caution. During the political campaign for reunification, many politicians claimed that the artificial boundaries set up by the mandate and trusteeship systems had divided members of the same tribe. Others who favoured the Nigerian connection pointed out that large groups had been divided by the Nigerian-Cameroon boundary, and they pointed to the Ekoi-Keyaka peoples of the Upper Cross River. The east-west boundary between the old French and British territories divided such groups as the Mbo, the Douala-Bakweri and the Bamenda-Bamileke groups.

While linguistically or culturally this is true we should point out that there were little or no 'tribal' feelings between different sections of these wider groupings. The Mbo, who lived in British Cameroons, had a legend of origin bringing them from Sandjo, a small Mbo village in French-speaking Cameroon, but that was as far as it went. The Bangwa of western Cameroon are linguistically and culturally related to the Bamileke chiefdoms of eastern Cameroon, but co-operation between chiefdoms was not very close and intermarriage infrequent. No 'tribal' consciousness among the Bamileke or Mbo could be said to have existed before colonial occupation, any more that there was a 'tribal' consciousness between Banyang in Cameroon and Ekoi in Nigeria.

The international boundaries, therefore, did not cut off 'brothers', although they certainly cut off political allies, trading partners and linked language groups as any boundary must do. It should be remembered that Bamileke, Mbo, Bamenda, Keyaka, Widekum, Bantoid, North-West Bantu are all names and concepts introduced by European linguists or administrators. It was the colonial and modern situation which in most cases made Cameroonian cultural groups aware of themselves.

CHAPTER 2

Mount Cameroon and the 'discovery' of Cameroon

The recorded history of Cameroon opens romantically with the very early discovery of Mount Cameroon by Carthaginian adventurers. This well-authenticated piece of history was in fact documented in stone. The leader of the Carthaginian expedition to West Africa, Hanno, commemorated his journey of discovery as far as Cameroon and Gabon by placing an inscription on the temple of Cronos at Carthage. From this inscription details of the fantastic journey became known to Greek and Roman authors. The date is not certain, but from the spectacular scale of the expedition it must have occurred during a period when the Phoenicians at Carthage were at the peak of their power. Thus with this valuable piece of historical material we know for a fact that Cameroon was discovered almost two thousand years before the arrival of the first European voyagers, the Portuguese, and that this discovery was made by an African.

However, Hanno was a North African, and he was also a colonialist, since the object of his journey was to found colonies beyond the Pillars of Hercules (Gibraltar). He sailed with sixty vessels – thousands of men and women and essential stores and equipment – along the desert coast of West Africa. He reached Senegal, where the hostility of the local inhabitants prevented a landing, and passed rivers full of crocodiles and hippopotamuses. He came to mountains covered with vegetation and landed on an island where his people were soon frightened off by fires and weird music. It was then, in Hanno's story, that the Carthaginian ships came to a land covered in streams of liquid fire flowing into the sea. This land – Cameroon – was inaccessible because of the heat, and – very much frightened – these North Africans hurried on. But for four nights they saw the land covered with flames and high overhead towered a fire greater than the rest which appeared to touch the skies. In the daytime they saw a huge mountain which they called the Chariot of the Gods.

Hanno recorded: 'We saw at night a land full of fire. In the middle

3 Old trade routes across the Eastern Sahara and Hanno's route to Mount Cameroon

was a lofty fire larger than all the rest touching seemingly the stars. By day this appeared to be a very great mountain called the Chariot of the Gods . . .' (Talbot, 1926, p. 347). Although Hanno's narrative is full of fantasy (his female savages with hairy bodies may have been gorillas), the story in the main, including the discovery of Mount Cameroon, can be taken as an accurate record.

Almost two millennia were to elapse before another effort to explore the coast is recorded, when Prince Henry the Navigator embarked on overseas exploration to capture the spices of the Far East and the gold of the West African Sudan via the sea. The explorations of Hanno may also have had commercial origins, for although the ancient writers are silent about Carthaginian trade with the interior of Africa, we have a lot of circumstantial evidence that the Carthaginians as well as the Romans traded overland with the Western Sudan.

CHAPTER 3

Cameroon and the Sudan

Northern Cameroon, as part of the great Chad basin, has been in intimate contact with political and cultural events of the Eastern Sudan and the Sahara at least from the early years of the Christian era. The Chad Basin is bordered by the Fezzan in the north, Tibesti in the north-east, Bagirmi in the south-east, Mandara and Adamawa in the south, the Bauchi plateau in the south-west and the Kouar and Djado in the west (see map on p. 10). It is an area in which the growth and decline of several flourishing cultures and state systems could be witnessed. The distribution of the Nok culture, which flourished around 200 BC, runs from Northern Nigeria (where it was first discovered during tin-mining operations) to the east of Lake Chad and west to the bend of the Niger. Nok culture, like the later Cameroonian culture we know as Sao, was almost entirely a pottery or terracotta art. During the first millennium after Christ, we see the growth and extension of the Kanem-Bornu empires and the Sao civilisation of Northern Cameroon.

Northern Cameroon is therefore an integral part of a region we know as the Western Sudan, a vast stretch of savannah land which runs from the western coast, in Senegal, through to Lake Chad in the east. It is an open region which has allowed the relatively free passage of migratory peoples (the Fulani are a spectacular example) and cultural movements, such as Islam. The region is well-described as 'orchard bush'; the north Cameroon savannah is studded with low trees and covered with grass during the summer rains. Towards Lake Chad we have thorn scrub and a thin grass cover which further north gives way again to stretches of bare rock and sand, typical of much of the Saharan desert. However, the habitable savannah lands of the Western Sudan do not stop at Lake Chad. The Western Sudan constitutes only the western part of a belt of open country which extends east to the Upper Nile and the Ethiopian highlands.

West African contacts with the African civilisations of the east have not so far been studied in such depth as have those with North Africa, but it is clear that Egyptian-type cultures spread into Ethiopia and further west in the third and fourth centuries A.D. The Nok and Sao civilisations of Northern Nigeria and the Cameroon, as well as probably most pre-Islamic empires of the Western Sudan owed many elements of their culture to eastern states, such as Cush, of the Nile valley. From the earliest dynastic periods Egypt was always in contact with the south, by both land and sea, and a thousand years before the birth of Christ, Cush, an African society, developed a culture inspired by Egyptian civilisation. Meroë, the capital, was founded later and became one of the largest iron-producing areas of the ancient world. From Meroë elements of this African culture, including the techniques of iron-working, spread into Ethiopia and along the savannah belt towards the Western Sudan. With it came a type of political organisation, associated with divine kingship, which remained typical of the old African kingdoms and empires of the pre-Islamic era.

The king, to whom divine powers were attributed, was typically secluded from the common people; he had to give audience behind a curtain and even his most intimate family, courtiers and servants might not see him eat or drink. The king was closely associated with the success of the crops and the fertility of his subjects and he performed innumerable rituals to ensure his own health and the well-being of the country. After the king's death – which was never considered a 'natural' one – the royal corpse was embalmed and the funeral ceremonies often involved the sacrifice of human victims. There was a bureaucracy of servants, while the pre-eminent offices were often those of the queen mother or sister, 'great wives' and powerful palace retainers. Many of these features of divine kingship indelibly marked many Cameroon state systems and survived in chiefdoms which still functioned in the twentieth century. Good examples are Nsaw of Bamenda, the Bamum and Bamileke chiefdoms of the Eastern Grassfields and the Kotoko kingdoms of northern Cameroon.

Iron-working played an important part in the growth and spread of state systems in the Western Sudan. Entering West Africa from the east and west, where they had been associated with priesthood as a source of power, the technical processes of the smith were, as far as possible, kept secret for a long period; and in some cultures they became confined to special families or castes. Today in the Cameroon smithing is often the prerogative of special social groups; and in Bamenda smiths have special offices in the royal bureaucracy. It is now believed that both divine kingship and iron-working were grafted on to the ancient Nok-type civilisations to produce such West African empires as Ancient Ghana, Kanem-Bornu and Sao. While details are lacking it is clear that, even before the invasions from North Africa in the tenth century and the introduction of Islam into the Western Sudan, the people of Northern Cameroon had already been in contact with immigrants and their culture from the east and north-east.

They had also, of course, been in contact with the west and the north. While the Sahara is a vast desert it has never been a complete barrier between southern countries, such as Nigeria and Cameroon, and the Mediterranean. All kinds of movements took place between West Africa and the Mediterranean from classical times to the 'Age of Discovery' when equatorial Africa was opened to Europeans from the sea. We had a glimpse of this in the account of Hanno's journey from Carthage down the West African coast. And throughout the first thousand years of the Christian era, until desert routes were outflanked by the sea, contact between the Western Sudan and the Mediterranean was constant and at times intensive.

The basis of these contacts was trade; Arabic writings revealed the importance of salt and gold in a two-way traffic between the north and the south. Great prosperity and the growth of complex states, such as Ghana, Kanem and Mali, came from this trade. There were three major routes across the desert; two of them, to the west, terminated in the great cities of Timbuktu and Kano. The route which directly concerned the Cameroon was that of Fezzan-Kawar-Bornu. The Fezzan-Kawar road was the old Roman road from the Garamantes to the 'Ethiopian' lands and its routes probably have not altered much since; it represented about two months' journey for a camel caravan. Roman generals, during the Roman occupation of North Africa, led their troops into the interior, occupied the Fezzan and, through this region, goods of the Sudan were sent to Roman markets. Herodotus mentions trading in the region and from his information it appears probable that the Tripoli-Kawar-Chad route was already in use at this time and that the northern part of the Cameroon was in some kind of contact with the classical world of the Mediterranean. The Carthaginians are known to have obtained 'carbuncles' (red precious stones) from the Garamantes and they were also provided with gold and slaves. Iron-working may have followed the same route.

However, neither Roman nor Carthaginian rule ever reached across the desert; the Carthaginian empire in particular was a commercial and maritime one; and as far as the Romans are concerned the oasis of Djerma (Garamantes) in the southern Fezzan marks the limit of their direct occupation, although commercial relations between the Mediterranean and the Western Sudan were significant. The importance of the Roman city Leptis Magna, close to modern Tripoli, suggests that it lay at the head of a major trans-Saharan trade-route running outwards through the Fezzan, to Lake Chad. The discovery of rock-drawings of horse-drawn vehicles along routes from the Fezzan support this since these drawings can only relate to ancient times.

Gold, ivory and ostrich feathers were exported from Chad to the Mediterranean along this important salt route. However, for hundreds of years the main commodity was slaves and the desert route became a blood-stained and skeleton-strewn road. Without the slave trade the rest of the caravan trade across to North Africa could hardly have existed, constituting as it did more than half or two-thirds of the value of the business conducted. The number of slaves exported to the north has been estimated at ten thousand a year, and many of those who travelled the eastern route and ended up in Tunisia, Turkey, Cyprus, even Albania, must have been Came-roonians captured during wars and razzias which accompanied the incursions of mounted warriors into the pagan areas of Northern Cameroon.

Many writers have pointed out that Africans were already used to slavery, employing slaves for their own use before the expansion of the desert trade and the Atlantic slave trade. Chiefs in the northern Grasslands of Cameroon were perhaps no exception. The two systems of slavery, European and African, were very different, however. African domestic slaves, palace slaves, were not used in plantations and did not have a purely economic value. They were valuable as retainers, servants, guardians of a chief's harem and as political followers. African chiefs turned war captives, criminals, witches into slaves; and usually the children of these slaves lost the status of slave and became attached to their father's owner in a client-patron relationship. Many slaves, retainers and clients of this kind could hold high posts in the households of the chiefs and their daughters often married royal princes, even producing heirs to the throne. An African slave was therefore a kind of kinsman with specific rights in the family. A slave bought from another group would be introduced into the domestic groups and attached to them. The slaves worked, married, brought their wives into the social group and formed part of the larger household.

Slavery in the Americas and in North Africa was primarily

economic. Slaves sent across the desert from the Chad area were mostly strong youths who left the region in good condition, coupled together by leg-irons and chained by the neck; women and girls walked free. Only the most robust of them survived the journey to the Fezzan where they were rested and fattened for the Tripoli market. It was a horrific trade although its horrors probably did not equal those of the European trade. During the Islamic period there was an even more enormous demand for slaves in North Africa, particularly eunuchs to work in royal harems – and raiding of the hill and forest pagans became one of the principal dry-weather occupations of the Muslim rulers and their warriors. Slavery was perpetuated in the name of religion throughout the length and breadth of the Western Sudan, and north Cameroon was no exception. Right across the sub-Saharan Africa from Chad to the mouth of the Senegal we find Sudanic kingdoms whose prosperity depended on the Saharan trade. Empires rose and fell according to the fluctuations of the trade, right up till the time of the Fulani *jihad* – or holy wars – of the nineteenth century. At the turn of the nineteenth century this important trans-African trade in goods and people ceased: decline and cessation were due to increasing insecurity and instability in the Sahara and the Sudan, the abolition of the slave trade in Tunis and in the Ottoman empire, and the successful drive of British, French and Germans up from the coast attracting trade goods towards the Atlantic.

CHAPTER 4

The Sao civilisation

The first known example of a Sudanic culture in Cameroon is that of the mediaeval kingdom of Sao. However, while Arab travellers recorded many details of the culture and organisation of empires such as Ghana, Mali, Songhai and Kanem, our knowledge of Sao civilisation comes only from archaeology and oral tradition. It grew up in the Chari delta, an area in north Cameroon which is open to all those diverse cultural influences which we have mentioned. Oral traditions are simple and bring the original Sao from the east. In fact they probably came in successive and diverse migrations, which would explain why different traditions hold them to have been dark-skinned or light-skinned.

On the whole it is accepted that Sao civilisation was authentically African, influenced by cultural currents from the Nile and the Mediterranean world. By the tenth century the Sao were well-established in the Chari Delta. They were remarkable in the whole Sudanic region for their lack of any warlike traditions and, probably for this reason, their country fell prey to invaders from the north, mainly from Kanem-Bornu, who attempted to wrest the land from them. By the end of the sixteenth century the Sao people and their culture disappeared until unearthed by archaeologists in the twentieth century.

For five hundred years or so, from the tenth until the fifteenth centuries, a great civilisation had flourished in north Cameroon south of Lake Chad. Their pottery, copper and bronze are all that remains of this remarkable culture. Terracotta was the most important medium for its artists and craftsmen – and funerary urns, jewellery and even money were made of this clay. Bronze artifacts which have been turned up by archaeologists include hoes, harpoons, fishhooks, knives and spearheads.

The Sao were conquered in the sixteenth century by a warlike people, known as the Massa, who entered the Chari region and settled

Examples of Sao pottery

alongside the Sao, intermarrying with them. The descendants of these two groups today form one people, known as the Kotoko, who live in a number of independent city states, the most important of which is Logone-Birnsi. Surrounded by larger empires to the west and east (Bornu and Bagirmi), the Kotoko paid tribute to them, although this did not prevent pillaging, particularly from Bagirmi, in the seventeenth century.

In the nineteenth century, as we shall see, the Logone-Birni were also invaded by the Fulani and other Nigerian peoples, who raided north Cameroon for slaves.

CHAPTER 5

The peopling of the Cameroon

From archaeology, oral traditions and classical and Arab writers, we have learned a little of the ancient history which affected the Cameroon. However, we have only touched on the fringes of Cameroon history proper. We shall learn much more when archaeologists and pre-historians turn their attention to this country; and already the discoveries of stone tools in Bamileke country, as well as at Maroua, Yaounde, Nsam and Ebobego, give us the first hints that most of Cameroon was occupied in very ancient times.

Unfortunately no general surveys have been made available of the archaeological work being done in the Cameroon and no positive statements can be made about early prehistory apart from the fact that the country has been occupied for a long period. Stone implements have been collected, which have been catalogued as either palaeolithic (old stone age) or neolithic (new stone age). These implements have been found throughout the region both at high and low levels, with some unusual concentrations in Bamenda. It has been suggested, on the basis of the form and material of these implements that the makers made their way down the Cross River valley. And for the history of the major population groups of the Cameroon, we have no real tangible records at all. Here we have to depend a good deal on the studies of linguists, who have been able to reconstruct, to a certain extent, the history of language groups, from their present-day geographical distribution and their inter-relationships.

Everyone knows that Africa is a 'Babel of tongues' – eight hundred is the number most commonly given, although it would be possible to make the number of African languages come out to almost any figure desired. This complexity, however, is only 'skin-deep' and linguists have been able to establish relationships between hundreds of languages and convert them into clusters of language families.

One American linguist (Greenberg, 1963) has clarified the situation by distinguishing four main language groups (see map on p. 20).

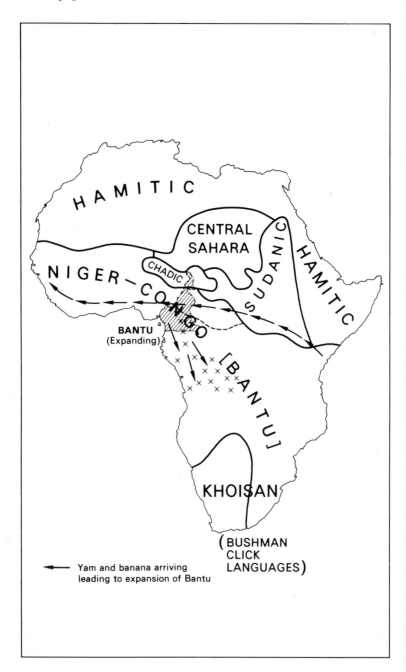

4 Four major language divisions

These are the *Click* languages of the Bushmen and Hottentot of South Africa, the *Sudanic* languages spoken by peoples of the Nile, the Western Sudan and the area of the Middle Niger River; the *Afro-Asiatic* group including Egyptian, Berber and some languages spoken around Lake Chad, the most important of which is Hausa; and the *Niger-Congo* group which covers the vast area from the Atlantic sea-board of West Africa to the eastern and southern edges of the continent.

In the Cameroon we should forget (or re-phrase) the myth that there are myriad languages, some as different from each other as Chinese from Icelandic. While there may be over seventy 'languages', they can all be classified into two of Greenberg's groups (the Niger-Congo and Afro-Asiatic groups) and the overwhelming majority of these fall into the former group. In northern Cameroon we have the only languages which do not belong to the Bantu section of the Niger-Congo group: these are those languages, related to Hausa, which are spoken by such groups as the Margi and Kapsiki. Their existence is clear proof of culture contact between this savannah region and distant north-east Africa.

All the other known forms of speech in the Cameroon belong to a single great group of languages, which we know as Bantu. The peoples of Cameroon and south-eastern Nigeria are the northernmost speakers of these languages and it is the historical implications of these facts which we are to discuss here.

Traditionally the Bantu language group in Cameroon is divided into two sub-groups, Bantu proper, spoken in the southern and south-eastern forest plains (Douala, Fang, Bakweri are examples) and the semi-Bantu (Bantoid) languages spoken in the western regions bordering Nigeria and the Central Highlands (Banyang and Bamileke). This broad division is convenient but it should not of course hide the fact that many of these 'languages' within 'language families' are very different and preclude any communications between speakers of different languages. This applies in the same way to the closely related Latin languages of southern Europe, which also belong to a closely linked 'language family' within the comprehensive Indo-European group which stretches from northern India to Great Britain.

Some students may immediately ask: what about the Fulani and the Pygmies? Are their languages not as distinctive as their cultures? The Fulani of Northern Cameroon speak a West Africa language of the same Niger-Congo group as Bantu. It is closely related to languages of Senegal from where they dispersed many hundred years ago. There are a few thousand pygmies left in eastern Cameroon – on the borders of Cameroon and Gabon, near the coast, and a single group in the savannah near Yoko. It is true that the Pygmies, probably the oldest occupants of the Cameroon, once spoke a non-Bantu language. Nowadays they no longer occupy separate tracts of land but are attached to particular Negro groups and speak the Bantu languages of these groups.

Language and race of course are quite separate. When we say that the Cameroonians are 'Bantu' or 'Chadic' we refer only to language, not to racial characteristics. There is no 'Bantu' race, as there is a European, a Negro or a Pygmy race. In Cameroon, apart from the Pygmies, there is only one clear racial division. There are no lines we can draw on a tribal map in order to claim that one group is more Negroid, another more Caucasoid. Even in the most dominant Negro tribes of the south there are to be found individuals with light skins and green eyes. Nor are the Pygmy groups completely pure since they have been indelibly mixed with their Negro neighbours. The Pastoral Fulani are often given as Caucasoids or Mediterraneans and it may be true that in some Fulani these strains predominate over Negro characteristics. However, the Fulani speak a language spoken by Negro groups and when they settled down to rule over conquered peoples as they did in their lamidats in Northern Cameroon, inter-marriage soon removes traces of their famous 'Caucasoid' characteristics.

What happened in history? Where did this vast family of Bantu speakers, who today people the forests and plains of sub-Saharan Africa, come from? The Congo forests and the vast regions of central and southern Africa were once occupied purely by scattered hunting groups like the Pygmies and Bushmen. At a certain period Bantu speakers swept into these empty lands and dispossessed these bands of hunters. The distribution of Bantu-speaking peoples from Cameroon to Southern Africa is so complete that it is assumed to be the result of peaceful expansion and repopulation, not conquest. This expansion was perhaps achieved through the combination of iron tools and new south-east Asian food crops – banana, cocoyams and yams – which enabled Bantu-speakers to wrest a comfortable living from the forest lands.

The problem before the historian is to discover the centre of origin of this dispersal. An English linguist (Guthrie, 1970) holds that the expansion and dispersal of Bantu farmers originated in a nuclear area south of the Congo forest. Guthrie has made an intensive study of Bantu languages and relationships and from these drew the conclusion that the original Bantu speakers lived in the equatorial forests midway between the east and west coasts of Africa. A more recent theory brings the first Bantu from the Cameroon and this theory, presented by the linguist, Greenberg, and the social anthropologist, Murdock, is fast gaining ground. According to them, Bantu-speakers of the Cameroon acquired the new south-east Asian food crops from East Africa along with iron farming tools. With these they entered the forest regions of the Cameroon, Gabon and Congo, increasing rapidly in numbers and displacing the hunting and gathering Pygmy peoples, of whom a few scattered remnants survive today. This movement extended from the central tropical forests into East Africa, penetrating Bushman country to the south and displacing them as it had earlier displaced the Pygmies. Cameroon, therefore, can be considered as the main cradle area for this explosion of Bantu-speakers from Nigeria to the Cape of Good Hope. The date suggested for the beginning of the migration is roughly two thousand years ago.

These are significant facts for the Cameroon and we should look a little closer at the deductions of linguists and anthropologists who have uncovered this information without written documents, the classical materials of the historian.

Of prime importance are the relationships between languages. If two peoples speak the same language, however much they differ in race and culture or however remote their geographical location, we can be certain that either they descended from a single group or the ancestors of one were in such intimate contact with the other that their original language was abandoned. This theory can be tested on European languages. English, for example, is spoken in Australia, West Africa and England. If we lacked written documents, how would we know that England, not Southern Nigeria or Queensland, is the home of the English language? This is done through linguistic relationships. English-speakers in Lagos have Yoruba-speakers for neighbours, and English-speakers in Sydney have Australian neighbours who speak aboriginal languages. None of these is related. The most closely related language to English is Frisian, then comes the Germanic group (Dutch, Flemish and German) and then the whole Indo-European family of which Germanic is a branch. The centre of dispersal for the English language (or languages) is therefore conclusively in north-western Europe.

The same theory can be applied to the Bantu question. How do we know that Cameroon, not Kenya or South Africa, is the original home of the Bantu language? It is reckoned that 2,500 years ago in the Cameroon area Bantu was a single language, spoken by a limited group. This hypothetical language we call Proto-Bantu. Then came the 'population explosion' (similar to the population explosion which sent the English language all over the world in the nineteenth century) and people from the Cameroon carried their language into the rain forests of the Congo and eventually all over Southern Africa. It can be shown that the language of the Tiv (Munshi) and others in the Central Benue region are most closely related to this Proto-Bantu language and it is probably somewhere in this region that the distributive centre is to be found.

Another study, known as glottochronology, which estimates the length of time languages have been separated from each other shows that Tiv and South African Bantu are distant by 2,000 years, another hint that the Bantu migrations began a century or two before the birth of Christ. Neighbours of the Tiv, the Ekoi of Cameroon, show a time gap of 3,000 years from Tiv. These hypotheses should be compared with the time gaps established between Frisian and English and American-English. English and Frisian, geographically as close as Ekoi and Tiv, have been separated for 1,500 years, American-English and English for only a few hundred.

The results of these linguistic studies show with little doubt that it is unlikely that the Bantu of Central and Southern Africa came from any region other than the Cameroon central highlands or a lowland region near the Cameroon-Nigeria area – the Benue-Cross River district.

Murdock, an anthropologist, has brought further ideas in support of this hypothesis, through his somewhat hypothetical studies of the origin of important South-East Asian food crops. According to him, the introduction of the yam and the banana into Africa in the era preceding the birth of Christ enabled Bantu speakers to exploit the forests of the hunting groups. The original Bantu group cultivated fonio, millet, sorghum – all crops which flourish only in the savannah. The introduction of the yam, the cocoyam and the banana provided the wherewithal for an African agricultural revolution. Murdock's argument is that these crops were brought into the Cameroon from East Africa, across the savannah belt (see map on p. 20). The Bantu hoe-cultivators who lived on the edges of the forest adopted the yam, the plantain and the cocoyam and Cameroon became the centre of a great agricultural revolution and the departure point for the Bantu peoples. This theory, however, has yet to be proved.

It should be remembered of course that the present inhabitants of Cameroon are not necessarily 'direct descendants' of these original immigrants. The Bantu have come and gone in this region in waves.

The Tiv moved out of their original homeland on the Cameroon border into north-eastern Nigeria. The Banyang (of the Ekoi group) have been migrating eastward over the past century or two. The Bamileke and Bamenda have a complex history of migration and counter-migration. The great Fang nation, for example, has reversed the hypothetical direction of Bantu migration, pushing southwards in fairly recent times into the south-east of Cameroon; they reached the coast and divided in two a group of Bantu speakers, the northern section of which we know as the North-west Bantu, the Douala, the Koko, the Kossi, Bassa, Bakweri and Kundu. The Fang movements coincided in east Cameroon with those of the Beti, both peoples being pushed south by the northern Wute. The Fang group includes the Ewondo, the Eton and the Bulu, and today there are a million Fang-Beti people distributed from the Sanaga to northern Gabon. Pahouin, Pangwe are other names for Fang. Charles Atangana, a famous Cameroonian, was a member of the Fang tribe.

Other Bantu speakers of west Cameroon, all of whom have recent traditions of migration into areas, include the Bakweri, Balong and Bambuko in Fako; the Bafo, Bakossi, Bakundu, Balong, Balundu, Basossi, Mbonge in Meme and Ndian and the Assumbo, Basossi and Mbo in Manyu. Kingkwa is a language spoken in the Bamileke-Mbo borderlands and provides a remarkable example of the fusion of a Bantu-Mbo and a semi-Bantu (Bangwa-Bamileke) language.

The Semi-Bantu

Semi-Bantu, as we saw, is a label given to most central Cameroon languages. It is a designation which really derives from the difficulty of connecting them or separating them from the major Bantu groups. Although called Semi-Bantu, they are probably the languages most directly linked with Proto-Bantu. The traditional label is nowadays a convenient means of separating them off as Bantu languages which have a considerable degree of Sudanic influence. In this Semi-Bantu group we find the Cross River languages of the Ekoi, Anyang, Banyang, Keyaka; and the Grassland languages of the Tikar, Mungaka, Bamileke and Bamum. The belt of Semi-Bantu languages is contiguous as can be seen on the map (see p. 7). However, the original language of the Bali, Mubako, which survives in Balikumbat, Bali Bagham and Baligasso is an Adamawa-Chamba language, thus betraying the Northern Cameroon origin of these intrusive nineteenth century invaders. Keyaka and Banyang speakers speak a similar language to the Ekoi of south-eastern Nigeria and share many cultural traits, such as their masked societies. Their languages are also related, but more distantly, to the Mbembe, Yakö and Ibibio peoples of Nigeria.

Pidjin English

Since Cameroon consists of many small tribes each with its own dialect or language, it is not surprising that a single language should be chosen as a *lingua franca* to help in communication between these diverse peoples. In the north both Hausa and Fulani are used. In Bamenda, Mungaka, the adopted language of the Bali, has a limited use as a vehicular language. In the south the trading superiority of the Douala led to their language being widely understood among their neighbours on the coast and also in the hinterland. Basel missionaries also used this language in their schools. However, it was a version of English, Pidjin English or Creole, which was used mostly between central and southern Cameroonians for trading purposes. Douala was discouraged by the German colonial administration and English became universal as a *lingua franca;* even the treaties between Germans and Douala were written in English.

Foreigners, on the whole, have provided the vocabulary, while the grammar, the word order, the intonation and the expressions are almost entirely based on local languages. Each tribe uses a different pidjin in the sense that they often translate some of their own language directly into pidjin. Pidjin English can be traced back to early European contacts with West Africa and has been used by traders, missionaries and colonial agents all over the West African coast. When Alfred Saker, the Baptist missionary, arrived in Fernando Po and later Fako, with his West Indian colleagues, a brand of Jamaican pidjin was introduced into Cameroon. For the Jamaican missionaries, this Creole English was their first language. Today it is the first language of many Cameroonians who are the children of parents from different cultures. Throughout the Cameroon it is a powerful and popular means of communication in the hands of church leaders, traders and politicians.

CHAPTER 6

Islam and the North

The southern migrations of many Bantu and Semi-Bantu groups within the last two centuries have been mainly occasioned by the movements and raids of northern warriors, primarily Fulani, looking for slaves and tribute-paying subjects. Many north Cameroon tribes, often called the 'Kirdi', sought refuge in inaccessible hill-country. Others moved south in search of peace and agricultural land. The Tikar, Bamileke and Fang migrations may all have been set off by northern slaving razzias, although the whole movement may have begun many centuries before the Fulani invasion of the eighteenth and nineteenth centuries. We saw that Kanem and Bornu warriors invaded and finally destroyed the Sao civilisation. Later the Chamba mounted warriors raided into Tikar lands in eastern Cameroon from Northern Nigeria. We shall consider the recent expansion of the Fulani as an example of these northern pressures before examining their effects in the central Cameroon – in Bamenda, Bamum and Bamileke country.

The Fulani provide a common theme in the history of most West African countries. They are a distinctive people, particularly in culture and physical appearance, and are found right across the Western Sudan from Dakar to the Gabon. Over this area – 3000 miles [4827 km] across – the Fulani pastoralists had slowly wandered, moving ever and ever further west, between the thirteenth and eighteenth centuries. They were – and some still are – simple cattle herders who sought pastures for their beasts further and further afield. Negro farmers, before the Holy Wars of the Fulani, lived in harmony with the Pastoral Fulani who were valued for their contributions to a purely agricultural economy.

The Pastoral Fulani remained pagans until the eighteenth century while all about them their Negro neighbours became converted to Islam. They even actively resisted the encroachments of Islam and organised opposition to missionary propaganda. However, in the

27

A Fulani woman

eighteenth and nineteenth centuries Islam began to take a hold and within a remarkably short space of time Fulani emirs had managed to carve out vast empires for themselves in the Western Sudan. Their history in each of these Sudanic states is remarkably similar.

In Cameroon today the Fulani number over 400,000. Their language, belonging to the Niger-Congo group, is different from Bantu but is closely related to languages spoken in Senegal (Serer and Wolof are examples) where the history of their phenomenal expansion begins. As we have seen, although they are said to look 'Caucasoid' or Mediterranean, their language is purely Negro and West African.

In fact it is some of their Negro subjects in Cameroon, along with the Hausa of Nigeria, who speak Chadic or Hamitic languages related to those spoken in north-east Africa and Arabia. The Fulani began moving into the Cameroon in the sixteenth and seventeenth centuries, seeking new pastures for their cattle and an escape from the financial demands of the Bornu princes.

Initially the Fulani mingled peacefully among the pagan population of north Cameroon, people who have generally been loosely classified together as the Kirdi. They inhabit the area of north Cameroon beyond the central plateau region and are primarily concentrated in northern sections of the western mountain regions and number about 800,000. They are in no sense a unified group, the Fulani word for 'pagan' (Kirdi) only being used to indicate their difference culturally from the Fulani and their non-Muslim neighbours. There are more than twenty-five such groups; the largest, like the Massa and the Mataka, have between 70 and 90,000 people, while others like the Kapsiki and Mofu have much less. As farmers they are distinct from their Fulani overlords. Many have been driven into isolated communities on the plains or in the mountains by Fulani invasions. Kirdi have always remained apart, and this, plus their remoteness from political centres, means that they have shared very little in the material progress taking place in Cameroon. Their areas are the least developed, although recent medical, educational and economic programmes have been undertaken.

Originally the Fulani were not fanatics and they did not hesitate to pay tribute to pagan chiefs or village heads. Towards the end of the eighteenth century the lamidats of Garoua, Rey and Bindir were established without any strife. However, from the beginning of the nineteenth century, the Fulani became militant missionaries of the Islamic faith and began to establish their presence in Northern Nigeria and Cameroon through conquest. As part of a large-scale Holy War (*jihad*) waged by Uthman dan Fodio against traditional chiefs, such as the Hausa, Fulani rule spread over larger areas of Nigeria and the Cameroon. Dan Fodio conquered much of Bornu-Kanem, for example, a state which had been in existence since at least the tenth century; he established the centre of his new empire at Sokoto, now in Northern Nigeria.

The Fulani empire was divided into separate units or fiefs under lieutenants of the great dan Fodio who had conquered separate regions. In Cameroon this lieutenant was Moddibo Adama, who came from the Benue River area.

In 1806 dan Fodio had called a meeting in Kano to discuss further conquests in the name of Islam. Many Fulani from present-day Adamawa were present, including Adama who was given the flag and sent to conquer the territory. Adama imposed his authority over other Fulani communities and led them against the unconquered pagan peoples, establishing himself at Yola. The first Fulani conquests were made in the north. Maroua was taken between 1808 and 1813, but they failed to conquer the western mountain area and the peoples of the banks of the Logone. They occupied the Diamare plain, and south of Maroua, they conquered Bindir in 1805 and Kalfa shortly afterwards. Some warlike indigenous peoples successfully resisted the Fulani incursions, while in the Guider region the *lamidos* preferred to establish their hegemony by peaceful means.

The Fulani overran the upper basin of the Benue between 1815 and 1820, except for the Fali of Kangu and the Tingilin. In 1820 two Fulani groups penetrated present-day Adamawa. Njobi installed himself at Ngaoundere. His successor made several expeditions into Kaka and Laka country in the region of the Pana Mountains, where he sought slaves. The lamido of Banyo, Haman Dandi, conquered the country north of the Mbam but was defeated at the hands of the Bamoun.

Towards the east of Ngaoundere the Gbaya people had been migrating into depopulated Mbum areas from the southern part of the present-day Central African Republic. Here a Fulani slaving column arrived from Ngaoundere after having forced the Mbum to submit. The Fulani were, of course, primarily interested in slaves, not conquest, and during the fifty years in which they consolidated their power prior to the arrival of the Germans, they sent out large annual military expeditions with hundreds of cavalry and thousands of foot soldiers, spending the dry season months raiding villages of the pagan peoples for slaves. From the Gbaya region, for example, slaves were taken to Ngaoundere where they were settled into farming villages on the land of their new masters, or sold to the north, or given as tribute to the emir of Yola, Adama, or his successors, his sons.

The Fulani enjoyed a clear-cut military success against all the poorly organised and armed peoples of Adamawa. Only those, like the Fali, who managed to flee, were not subdued and decimated. The Mbum, for example, fought back vigorously when the Fulani raids began, fighting from entrenched positions on the steep hills, but they were consistently defeated and incorporated into the Fulani system. The Gbaya, on the other hand, never became vassals of the Fulani, since the scattered clan groups refused to submit to their control. Instead the Gbaya made alliances with the Fulani, agreeing to pay

The lamido's palace

them slaves and ivory, thereby becoming slave raiders for the Fulani.

However, Fulani dominance and explotiation of local peoples lasted a relatively short time. With the arrival of the Germans at the end of the nineteenth century their power was immediately curtailed. Originally Fulani government was centred in Sokoto and the sultan was overlord of the emir of Yola, who in turn had his vassal princes, the north Cameroon lamidos. When the Germans came they retained the Fulani organisation, with the exception that the local lamido ruled through a resident German adviser. Today there are twenty-one *lamidats* (the territory ruled by a lamido) in northern Cameroon, the most important of which are Garoua, Maroua and Ngaoundere.

The Fulani invasions and conquests changed the face of the north in the early nineteenth century. The basis of the Fulani economy was slavery and slaves were continually taken from the plateau peoples in razzias or delivered as tribute to the Fulani chiefs by pagan chiefs. In Bamum, to the south a slave was worth the price of a goat, but he would be sold for 33,000 cowries, or the price of a horse at Sokoto. The emir of Yola, every year, received five thousand slaves. Following on the heels of the Fulani came the Hausa traders, who entered the region to exploit trade goods such as ivory, wild pepper and kola. These merchants represented long-distance Hausa trading networks stretching throughout northern Cameroon and into Northern Nigeria. They also acted as useful political agents for the Fulani lamido. Goods traded south by the northern traders included cottons, glass beads, scent, embroidered clothes, salt, iron and copper bars. The monopoly of trade which the Hausa traders had secured was, of course, broken by the introduction of foreign trading houses in the Niger and Benue regions after 1880.

Islam

While the Holy Wars of dan Fodio aimed at introducing Islam into Nigeria and the Cameroon by force, this religion had previously been brought into the country much earlier than the conquest period. Originally all the inhabitants, including the Fulani cattle-herders themselves, had been pagans and, although Fulani dynasties were founded in the eighteenth century, many of the tribes were unaffected by Islam until the nineteenth and twentieth centuries. Islam was first introduced by traders and their activities in purveying Islam along with their goods continued after the Fulani conquests and the formation of theocratic states when many Africans were forcibly converted. It is a religion which unlike Christianity adapts easily to African ways of thought and African social organisation: their polygyny and bride-wealth, for example, are not accepted by Christians but they are part and parcel of Islamic systems. Nevertheless among many pagan tribes, particularly those who fled to isolated areas when the Fulani invasions occurred, Islam made very few inroads.

In Cameroon today Muslims must number a million people. Islam has penetrated most of the northern parts of eastern Cameroon. Apart from people who belong to wholly Muslim groups such as the Shuwa Arabs (25,000), the Kotoko, the Bornuans and the Hausa and those who are partially Islamicised, such as the Bamum, Tikar, Wute and Gbaya, there has also been a certain amount of penetration among the Fali (Mongo), the Nsaw and the Bamileke.

Rabeh

All kinds of influences, in terms of people and culture, have been felt in north Cameroon from the east. In the north, for example, there are a few scattered 'Arab' tribes, some of them particularly around Bornu known as the Shuwa. They are mostly cattle-nomads and represent a very early (probably seventeenth century) migration of Muslims from the Sudan. Although they have lost many of their Mediterranean traits through intermarriage with Negroes, the Arab element is clearly recognisable.

A more recent connection with the east was the reign of Rabeh, a colourful slave raider and adventurer from the Nile regions who carved out his own state to the north of Cameroon. Rabeh entered the service of Zobeir Pasha, the Governor of the Bahr-el-Ghazal, to the south-east of Lake Chad, in 1870. While his master was in Egypt, Rabeh rebelled and with fifty soldiers moved westwards conquering all the tribes between the basins of the Nile, the Chari and the Ubangi. From 1880 to 1895, he exploited the occupied zone, extending his power, defeating the Bagirmi and reaching as far as the lower Chari. His empire included Bornu, parts of Bagirmi and his capital was at Dikwa. With the arrival of the French and the battles that ensued Rabeh was at first successful but was later defeated. He was killed and thrown in the Chari before the French occupied his capital in 1900. In the early colonial period the French ruled Rabeh's empire through members of the old Kanem dynasty whom Rabeh had defeated.

CHAPTER 7

The Central Cameroon Highlands

The pressure of northern raiders, such as the Fulani, seeking slaves and subjects had important effects to the south, among the Tikar, Bamum, Bamileke and Bamenda peoples. The well-known Tikar movements from north-eastern Cameroon, southwards and west-wards into the Bamileke and Bamenda Grassfields were a direct result of these razzias. The raids of mounted Fulani in east Cameroon led to the southern migration of the Mbum. And the Mbum pressure in turn caused the southward expansion of the Babute or Wute, who forced the Fang and Beti to begin their long migration towards the coast. In the nineteenth century the Chamba-Bali arrived in the Grassfields area; like their enemies, the Fulani, these mounted horse-men sought subjects and trading opportunities in un-exploited terri-tories. The Bali contributed in no small way to the atmosphere of movement and change which characterised the Bamenda Grassfields at this time.

In this section we shall look at the history, as well as some of the traditional institutions, of the major peoples of this central region. The Grassfields, a relatively open country, stretches from Widekum in west Cameroon, to the north-eastern savannah plains which con-tinue beyond Foumban, the capital of Bamum. It is a zone of ancient forest clearance which runs across the Republic from east to west between the fourth and seventh parallels. In west Cameroon it is marked off from the Upper Cross River basin – the Mamfe de-pression – by a sharp escarpment, and from the middle basin of the Katsina Ala River, by a range of hills running to the north-east. In the north it is marked off from Takum and Adamawa by mountain ranges (see map on p. 35). The region is a relatively fertile high plateau. On the south-eastern side of the Bamenda plateau, we find the Ndop plain which is continuous with the Mbaw Plain to the north-east in east Cameroon. Open country has allowed widely scattered compounds, surrounded by farms – as well as ease of move-

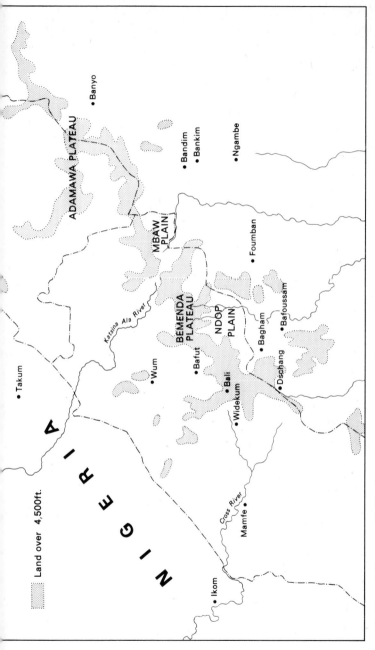

5 The Central Cameroon Highlands

ment for migrants and invaders.

On the whole the peoples of the region form a homogeneous culture area, speaking related Semi-Bantu or Bantoid languages and sharing institutions. Nevertheless there are different groups, such as the Banen and Bafia to the east of the Bamileke, and enclaves of heterogeneous peoples in parts of Bamenda. In Bamenda there are people with matrilineal institutions living as close neighbours of villagers who speak a similar language but practise patrilineal inheritance and succession. In Kom, for example, the second largest kingdom in Bamenda with a population of 30,000, succession to the chiefship is to the ruler's sister's son, while among the Nsaw, succession is universally patrilineal.

Throughout Bamenda and the Eastern Grassfields there are common themes. Chiefship is almost universally important and kingdoms range from a few hundreds to tens of thousands. In all of them men's associations ('secret societies', military groups) played an important part in the social organisation. Some societies, often composed of high-ranking retainers, judged disputes and punished crimes against the state. *Manjong* was an association to which all adult males belonged and whose functions were military. The chief, who had sacred attributes, was the head of a complex body of palace and state title-holders, usually supported by a 'queen mother' or a 'queen sister'. Divination – by the earth spider – is common in the area and so are ancestor cults. The whole of central Cameroon also shares a similar attitude to the birth of twins who are universally honoured and feared.

Building styles and art styles are also shared across this central plateau region with some diversification. In the forest region, house styles are mostly low rectangular huts roofed with palm thatch. In Bamenda and the Eastern Grassfields houses are tall, square huts with pyramidal grass-thatched roofs. In the palaces of chiefs there were remarkable royal and ceremonial buildings, panelled with raffia bamboos or woven 'mats'; they can still be seen at Bafut, Mankon and Fontem. Society meeting-halls with carved door surrounds and pillars can be seen at Kumbo. Weaving crafts were highly developed and the dress of Bamenda notables – in embroidered gowns, pleated kilts and elaborate hats – is a splendid affair. Weaving, hat-making, tailoring, sculpturing are all crafts which are done by men. Pottery, however, particularly in the chief centres – the Ndop towns of Nsei, Bamungo and Bamessi – is the work of women. Here they make large cooking pots, smaller pots with relief decoration and jars with animal ornaments and high relief. These pots are frequently covered with a black glaze made of soot or graphite mixed with plant extracts.

A carved door surround in Central Cameroon

Metal crafts in western Cameroon have been carried on for a long time. Oral traditions of several peoples refer to the arrival of smiths, and smiths as makers of the famous gongs of the secret societies are favourite figures in many foundation legends. For example, the smiths of Babungo, as well as the Ti smiths of Bali Nyonga, claim like the Fali that their ancestors fell from heaven.

Working of bronze, by the lost wax method, is a famous craft among the Tikar, Bamum and Bagam of east Cameroon, although it was not practised in the Bamenda area in pre-colonial times and most of the royal brass treasure was imported from the east. Spears, other weapons, agricultural instruments, knives, copper bangles were all made. Throughout the Grassland area, sculpture – in the form of masks, ancestor figures and architectural ornament – is highly developed, although within the general Grasslands' style there is a great diversity of techniques and approach.

Music of diverse and highly developed kinds is found throughout the Cameroon. Xylophones (either with gourd as sound-box, or with keys laid across banana stems), Bali gourd trumpets, flutes and gongs of many kinds are often formed into orchestras, played by secret societies. Famous gongs (they are really iron bells) were made in Fontem and in Kom. Drums of many kinds are to be found, the most impressive being the huge slitgongs drummed at the death of a chief's son or daughter.

Bali trade, particularly in slaves, brought prosperity to many Bamenda chiefdoms and was the motive behind the movements of groups of mounted horsemen – such as the Bali-Chamba – disturbing the peace of the highland plateau. Slaves were sent by Bamenda traders towards Calabar in exchange for European goods such as salt, guns and cotton. In this way goods which were once luxuries, such as spirits, cloth, tobacco and beads, became necessities. Imports were also paid for in ivory and later, rubber, while further south, palm oil had increased in value as an export after the official abolition of the slave trade in 1808. Manchester cottons became an important item of Grassfields trade in the nineteenth century and even Cheshire salt came out from Britain as ships ballast and led to the decline of local salt mines. Local tools and weapons were also replaced by those made in Birmingham.

Throughout the Cameroon, but particularly in this central region, there were several trade currencies – any convenient, divisible import was accepted as a unit of trade currency, and all exports and imports were then valued in terms of this unit. Manillas, cowries, copper rods, salt, cloth, all became in turn accepted as the local currency.

In the central Cameroon elaborate palace administration, large polygynous compounds, luxurious courts were all supported by this important trade. In the main it was carried on through forest middlemen. The Bamenda peoples, for example, traded their slaves primarily through Banyang intermediaries. The Bamileke used both Bangwa, Mundani and Banyang middlemen – or Bakossi and Mbo if they traded southwards. The Bali, Bafut, Nsaw, Bamum and Bamileke chiefdoms were linked as allies in this trade and sometimes as competitors. Profits gave the Fons (chiefs) the wherewithal to support retainers, clients, wives, craftsmen and royal militias.

The Tikar
Obviously, it is impossible to take into account the many different oral traditions and legends which describe the arrival of different groups in Cameroon. There are so many of them, ranging from purely mythical accounts of an original founder – a smith – a hero,

who came from a hole in the ground, to down-to earth historical accounts of the dynastic legends of the Tikar. According to their own traditions, the various groups of Tikar settled in Bamenda, originally came from Tibati, Banyo, Kimi and Ndobo – all in north-east Cameroon. One Tikar group migrated further south and south-west to settle between latitudes 6 and 8 North in a savannah-like country, still called the Tikar Plain and still inhabited by remnants of the original migration. Kimi Manga, the present Bankim, apparently became the political centre of this Tikar group.

It was about three hundred years ago that increasing pressure from the north and internal troubles, plus the desire for new lands led to the splitting up of Tikar groups into small bands, which having left Kimi, drifted further west and south-west. Some of these moved under the leadership of the sons of a Tikar ruler who later called themselves Fons, the most common Bamenda term for paramount chiefs. These groups, at various times, reached what is now Mezam. Among the earlier were those who came from Ndobo to the Ndop plain in the south of Bamenda, where they formed small, politically independent villages a few miles apart. No semblance of political unity was achieved. In the north-east we have Mbaw, Mbem and Nsungli, also settlements of Tikar, and below the escarpment at a later date, settlements of Wiya, Tang and War. The main body of this group, however, set off under the leadership of their Fon and founded the kingdom of Bum. The Bafut, Kom and Nsaw were among the last to arrive.

Bamum traditions of origin bring a small princely emigrant group from Rifum, or modern Bankim, (another traditional centre of dispersal in the region of the Upper Mbam River) who settled among the chiefdoms which were already flourishing. The Nsaw story brings a Rifum (Tikar) prince through the Mbaw Plain to Kovifem on the plateau where they made their first capital. During the Kovifem period the Nsaw population was enlarged by the arrival of settlers, but attacks from the north drove the dynasty to Kumbo in the 1820s. Today Nsaw is the largest of the Bamenda chiefdoms, with a population of over 105,000. The capital is Kumbo (or Kimbaw) and has a population of over 5,000 and is surrounded by a number of attached villages. It is the political hub of a densely settled area. Within the chiefdom there are refugee chiefs and conquered chiefdoms which retain their hereditary dynasties. Nsaw is remarkable for its elaborate political structure; and the differentiation between ranking chiefs, royal princes and princesses, royals of different classes, free commoners, retainers and servants expresses one aspect of this political complexity.

During the nineteenth century five kingdoms with Tikar or Ndobo derived dynasties, Nsaw, Kom, Bafut, Bum and Ndu, extended their boundaries by incorporating, or making tributary, neighbouring village chiefdoms. Bum, though small, was important since it was the entrepot for the kola trade with Jukun and Hausa in the north-west, during the later part of the century. It was on terms of intermittent hostility with its southern neighbour Kom, but had pacts of friend-ship with Nsaw and Ndu. Nsaw, for the most part, was at logger-heads with Ndu, but had an alliance with Kom, while Kom competed with Bafut on its south-western boundary for the allegiance of tiny village chiefdoms.

The Bamenda States

The political structure of the Bamenda chiefdoms – Bafut, Bali, Tikar, Kom, Bum – and those of the Bamileke Grassfields were basically similar. Nsaw provides an example of this traditional gov-ernment, which contrasts with the political organisation of the Wide-kum, Mbembe and forest peoples, where the village was the political unit and the village head had very little executive authority. In Nsaw, as in most of the Grassfields chiefdoms, there was a sacred kingship, a cult of dead kings, a distinction between royals and commoners, certain titles reserved to princes and princesses, state councillors (usually hereditary) and a military organisation based on village or ward warrior lodges.

In Nsaw much of the political structure is intact. The villages of alien origin which were conquered by invading Tikar in the last century became tributary to the Fon of Nsaw, but they maintained a degree of independence in the management of their own affairs. The Fon has his palace at Kumbo comprising his own inner court-yards, dwelling huts, kitchen, stores, a large courtyard where the Fon hears cases, another flanked by the houses of his wives and the head-quarters of the palace secret society.

The management of the palace, the guardianship of the Fon's wives and the control of food and wine supplies are looked after by palace officials who live near the palace. The Fon's big councillors are the *vibai*, and the high priest and priestess and queen mothers also assist in government and hear cases. Upon the succession of a Fon the title of queen mother is conferred upon his mother, or, if she is dead, upon a 'sister' or daughter.

In the old days the Fon, like all Bamenda chiefs, had his military organisation, each village having its own club house. Adult men all belonged and met regularly for drinking, hunting, or giving military services when called upon to do so. Today these societies no longer have military functions, but still exist for purposes of recreation. A distinctive feature of the political system of all Grassland states was the police society known as *ngwerong, kwifon, menang, tro* or *ngumba*, which usually had its quarters in the palace precincts and had among its duties the recruitment in boyhood of palace retainers from free-born commoners. It was the executive arm of government and could therefore be regarded as a body of recruited retainers.

In Bamileke chiefdoms it was always a secret society with sacred gongs and special ritual functions. There were important masks associated with it. One day in the eight-day week was reserved for it: members met and no-one else in the capital might fire a gun or strike a drum on pain of punishment. At important national events or the death of a member, the society put on its masked dances. In the execution of its state duties, its retainers appeared clothed in net gowns which masked face and body; its authority was of an impersonal kind and its agents could not be held to account by the populace. It was everywhere seen as supporting the chief – without it there would be disorder.

Bamum

Perhaps the most famed and certainly the largest of the Grasslands' kingdoms is Bamum. The first Bamum immigrants settled among the Bamileke chiefdoms who then occupied most of present-day Bamum. From Foumban their chief, Nchare, fought and defeated the Bamileke, setting himself up as their overlord. The Bamum then had to deal with the southward-raiding Fulani, who at first defeated them and destroyed their capital at Foumban. It was rebuilt, however, and provided with huge ditches and fortifications against future Fulani raids. The boundaries of Bamun eventually reached the Noun River in the west and south-west and the Mbam in the east. Its population today is over 100,000. The conquered Bamileke either left the territory – moving across the Noun or in the direction of Bali and Nsaw in West Cameroon – or accepted the suzerainty of the Bamum king.

The Bamum state had many elements in common with Nsaw, although some institutions were distinctly original. There was an important duality running through society which was determined by the fact that two categories of persons were distinguished – the descendants of kings (and royals were innumerable after two hundred years of power and polygyny; the royal lineage had countless collateral branches) and the king's servants, recruited from prisoners of war, foreigners who sought the king's protection, and the descendants of servants and former slaves. Although the royal princes in Foumban provided an heir to the throne, they were excluded from any participation in administration or policy-making. Servants and retainers were the councillors of the king and administered the country although, of course, they had no right to the supreme functions of kingship.

This system, or variations of it, is found all over the Eastern Grassfields; royals possess wealth, prestige and title, but all political influence is handed over to important commoners and retainers who hold vital administrative and governmental posts.

One of the greatest personalities of Cameroon history was the old king of Bamum, Njoya. In about 1885 his father was killed in the Nsaw war and at the age of four he was chosen to succeed. His mother acted as regent until he was old enough to take over the reins of government himself. Njoya, a highly intelligent and original prince, determined to expand the prestige, if not the boundaries, of his kingdom; he fought in vain against the Germans and when he tried to prevent French colonial penetration his efforts led to his deportation to Yaounde where he died in 1933.

Njoya built the splendid and original palace at Foumban. It is a vast structure adorned with sculpted columns and panelled walls; it has innumerable courtyards where the Sultan's wives live in seclusion under the care of royal retainers. Njoya was open to all new ideas: after toying with Christianity, he finally adopted Islam. He also encouraged the cultural development of his people who were, and are, experts in bronze-working, wood-carving and weaving. The Sultan patronised local crafts in order that his people should not forget their own culture in face of the competition of easily purchased European articles. In Foumban there is a museum for the preservation of past works of art and the paraphernalia of royal societies and war associations (*manjong*). There is also a whole street devoted to these traditional crafts which still flourish in Bamum.

Njoya also developed a system of writing which shares, with that of the Vai of Liberia, the honour of being the only Negro scripts ever invented. When first observed in 1902 by Germans, the Bamum were using 348 signs, largely ideographic and pictographic. Njoya had heard of German writing and knew of the Arabic script of the Hausa traders. He wanted to communicate secretly with his local officials, so he called a meeting of his council and proposed the creation of a form of writing. Since the language consisted largely of monosyllabic roots the original signs were readily converted in 1909 into a syllabary.

The Sultan of Bamum standing outside his palace

After further developments it was made into a true alphabet. He also wrote an impressive history of his dynasty and his country in the new script.

The Bamileke

'Bamileke' is a convenient administrative term 'invented' by the Germans for the inhabitants of a hundred or so chiefdoms scattered across the Grassfields of eastern Cameroon south of the kingdom of Bamum. Most of the dynasties of the Bamileke chiefdoms derive from the north, whence they were chased by the Fulani and the Bamum. They crossed the Noun and settled in their present general location. The Baleng were, perhaps, the first to cross the Noun, followed by the Bandeng and Bapi. The Bafoussam came next and settled south of the Baleng.

The history of these Bamileke chiefdoms and their numerous offshoots is considerably difficult to untangle today. Baleng, for example, is the original ancestor of the Bandjoun, Bafang and Bangangte; the Bamendou dynasty founded Baham and Bangou. Yet many Bamileke chiefdoms, particularly those in the west, have no direct links with the north but derive their ancestors from original inhabitants or even from forest villages of the Mbo and Banyang. There is a degree of inter-mingling between Bamileke and their forest neighbours and the tendency is for Bamileke culture and language to replace those of the forest peoples who move up towards the Grassfields. Bamileke number 750,000 inhabitants mostly living in the plateau areas to the south and east of the Bambuto mountains. A complex of small chiefdoms, comprising five main areas which are around Dschang, Mbouda, Bafang, Bafoussam and Bangangte. The largest chiefdom has more than 30,000 inhabitants and others have less than a thousand.

The Bamileke chiefdoms, like those in Bamenda, are ruled over by a Fon. The chiefdoms were completely independent and even in their own chiefdom, there were sub-chiefdoms with varying degrees of autonomy, depending on whether they were sub-chiefdoms of the paramount through conquest, voluntary allegiance. etc. A chief ruled with the help of various councils and associations formed of titled retainers, princes and commoners. The *kamveu*, the most important, was a group of nine councillors who advised on matters of importance. Other societies performed religious, military or occupational functions and there were also age groups organised in war socieities.

A striking factor about the Bamileke is their passion for independence; royals and title-holders continually break away from their parent chiefdoms and overlords to set up their own little states in relatively sparsely populated regions to the south and west. When the Germans arrived, there were a host of small chiefdoms, although one, Bandjoun, had begun to extend its power over some groups to the west.

Movement among the Bamileke is constant; this is particularly due to population pressure which over the last forty years has increased at a great rate, and land shortage has become serious. The system of inheritance to a single heir meant that other sons were left with no land resources unless they could acquire some from the chief, the titular owner of the land of a Bamileke chiefdom. Large numbers of Bamileke sought employment in towns, or migrated and settled south in lands where the area could be farmed. In the Mungo regions, for example, they hired themselves out as labourers, then acquired farms and brought their families to live there. Their commercial success brought them trouble after independence, including conflict with

A Bamileke chief

local peoples who feared the Bamileke were expropriating their land through trickery.

Another misfortune hit the Bamileke after independence when they found that they did not gain the political plums they had hoped for; their reactions in protest led to violent reprisals on the part of the new government. We shall see later to what extent. Both local Bamileke and town Bamileke took part in the revolt organised by the UPC (Union des Populations du Cameroun). In the 1940s an attempt was made to found an allegedly traditional pan-Bamileke organisation, known as the Kumze, but there is no historical basis for this association. It did, however, provide a means for Bamileke to associate outside the chiefship framework.

In west Cameroon there is a group of nine Bamileke chiefdoms, the Bangwa, which were cut off from their cultural neighbours by the administrative boundaries drawn up by the French and English after the defeat of the Germans in the first world war. The Bangwa

45

occupy the escarpment between the savannah region of east Cameroon and the Banyang and Mbo forests of the west. They speak languages akin to their Dschang neighbours and share the general Bamileke characteristics which have become famous throughout the Cameroon. They have a highly individual and expert art style; their leaders were both wealthy, 'many-wived' chiefs and progressive traders who adapted with alacrity and success to opportunities offered by the outside world.

Other Bamenda groups

In Bamenda the picture is not as straightforward as it is in eastern Cameroon. Here the language and cultural situation is much more heterogeneous, possibly due to the proximity with widely differing people in Nigeria. For example, we have groups of 'matrilineal' peoples – Fungom, Wum, Kom and Aghem – which share institutions involving inheritance and succession from mother's brother to sister's son. Since they exist in close proximity to villages with patrilineal institutions, the indications are that matriliny, associated with peoples to the north and west is dying out and being replaced by the more common patrilineal institutions found throughout the Grassfields. In Aghem the town is divided into six sections; five of these are long established and have matrilineal dynasties apart from one which claims 'Munshi' origin. The language of Aghem is very closely related to that of Fungom. All the groups seem to have been raided by slavers from the Katsina Ala valley in the last decades of the nineteenth century.

The Bafut dynasty, like so many others, claims origin from Ndobo, in northern Bamum and the Upper Mbam. But the chiefdom is a composite one. In the Ndop plain, apart from the Bali-Chamba settlements, there are eleven village chiefdoms. Papiakum derives from Bamum recently. Other villages moved into the plain as a result of Foumban pressure (Bangola and Bafanji). Bamessi claims Ndobo origin. The Babungo dynasty has a myth of origin which brings the first chief from a cave behind a waterfall. The Babungo smith fell from heaven, his hammer in his right hand and started a craft for which Babungo is still famous. Its neighbour Bamessing (also famous for iron-working) has a king-list of 26 but a mid-nineteenth century Fulani raid disrupted the kingdom and dispersed many of its elements far afield.

The Widekum and Mbembe

Another Bamenda group is that of the 'Widekum' (the Ngemba,

Ngie, Ngwo, Mogamo, Meta, Esimbi and Beba Befang) who are grouped together because they usually give the village of Widekum on the Manyu border as the place from which they migrated to Bamenda. The mythical site of origin for many of these south-western Bamenda village dynasties is Tadkon, some two and a half miles [4 km] south of the present palace of the chief of Batibo. Here there are places associated with the emergence from the earth of the primal ancestor Mbeka, and an old market site containing the stone back-rest of clan heads, said to have dispersed from Tadkon south to Widekum, north to Mankon and north-west to the Meta villages by many routes. The Mogamo villages do not all claim Tadkon origin, some claiming connections with Mbu, others with the Mundani. The traditions of the area like those of the related Mundani seem to point to a slow movement of small groups to and from the important palm-oil line.

Mankon, the largest chiefdom, has a long king-list of twenty-one ancestors. The present site of Mankon dates from the early part of the nineteenth century when they defended themselves against the Bali-Chamba and enclosed the capital in a system of moats and river defences.

The Mbembe group, which includes the Misaje and Mfumte, has diverse traditions of origin. Mfumte traditions bring some village ancestors from 'Fumban'. The majority of Mbem villages, however, claim an origin in Kimi (Tikar) country. Both the Mbem and Ntem areas were heavily raided for slaves by the Banyo lamidat. The Ntem chiefdom has preserved a tradition of Kimi origin, and beyond that to Mbum and Bornu. Mbembe traditions of origin are also very mixed: some bring sections of the people from the north-east, others from 'Munshi', from the north-eastern Nigerian borderland. Perhaps also many of the inhabitants arrived – under Chamba or Fulani pressure – in the first half of the nineteenth century.

The 'Widekum', along with most Mbembe and Mogamo peoples, do not have elaborate state structures like those described for the Nsaw. Here the lineage organisation provides the framework of the political structure. Clans tend to be localised in villages, and as a rule most of the lineages in one village are segments of the patriclan of the village head. Thus, unlike the mixed villages of Nsaw and the other Grassland chiefdoms, these villagers could be said to be all of one family. Usually one lineage is senior to the others and its head acts as a village head. Once upon a time it is said that members of such a clan could not marry, but now intermarriage is permitted among and between some of these neighbouring lineages. Each lineage in a village of this kind has under its control a tract of arable land which the head hands out to individuals. A lineage head looks after members in many ways, performing sacrifices, and has a right to a portion of game when they hunt. But he has nothing comparable with the economic privileges of a Tikar chief or lineage head.

In Bamenda in the matrilineal groups (Kom, Aghem and five Fongom villages) the matrilineage does not live together, since men choose to reside with their father after marriage (not their mother's brother) or even with an in-law or a friend. The lineage has some functions, usually in a ritual and advisory capacity. Among the Kom and Fungom, he usually has a tract of residential and arable land under his control, which he gives out to his kin. In theory these matriclans are exogamous units, but marriages sometimes occur when the parties belong to different lineages living in different villages.

The Bali

The Bali are relative newcomers to the Grassfields, but their history, recorded in some detail (Kaberry and Chilver, 1968), provides an illuminating illustration of the political pressures and military raids which produced the rather turbulent picture of Bamenda in the eighteenth and nineteenth centuries. At the beginning of the nineteenth century an Adamawa people, the Chamba, suffered famine and pressure from their neighbours as well as the first movements of Fulani mounted raiders in the region of the Upper Benue. The Chamba, with their horses, moved out to seek regions where there was food and, if possible, tribute-payers to provide it. They, like the Fulani, were slave-raiders but travelled south to exchange their interest in northern slave markets for the distant markets of the southern forests which provided European needs and the growing demand for slave labour in the new palm oil plantations.

The Bali-Chamba moved south through east Cameroon, where they were joined by contingents of the warlike Tikar, Wute and Mbum, and one Bali band raided into the Western Grassfields of central Cameroon. Around 1835 they were defeated at Bafou-Fondo near Dschang in east Cameroon by an alliance of Bamileke chiefdoms. By 1850 they were in Bamenda where they established settlements and competed with the already established city states of Mankon and Bafut for the adherence of smaller villages.

In the first period of Bali-Chamba settlement, Bali-Kumbad was the dominant state, and the arrival of Bali-Nyonga in the far west of the Grassfields area may well have been due to a desire to escape its influence and pressure. Zintgraff, the leader of the first German exploratory party from the south, was the first European to arrive in the area in 1889 and Bali-Nyonga became a station of the German administration and German trading companies. The Chamba language spoken at Bali-Nyonga was abandoned in favour of Mungaka, a kind of pidjin Bamileke picked up by the Bali on their excursions in the Eastern Grassfields. It has received a wide use owing to its adoption by the Basel Mission after 1903. In the eastern Bali-Chamba settlement the original language still holds its own, presumably because the original Chamba elements were larger.

CHAPTER 8

The coastal peoples

History in the south remains unrecorded between the discovery of Mount Cameroon by Hanno, the Carthaginian, and the arrival of the Portuguese in the sixteenth century. Apart from oral traditions recorded for the Douala, Bakweri, Fang, and other Bantu peoples of the region, our historical pages for this period are a blank.

The inhabitants of the coastal regions of Cameroon are known as the North-West Bantu and with them the Bantu languages of Africa reach their farthest extension at the African coast. The recent migrations of these people are in no sense a continuation of the more ancient Bantu movements described in an earlier section; in fact the general movements up from the Congo and down towards the coast are the reverse of the trend of earlier movements. The traditions of the Douala, in fact, bring their ancestors from the south, from the equatorial Congo Basin.

The ultimate ancestor of the Douala is said to have been named Mbongo. A son or descendant of his was Mbedi, the father of Ewale, the direct ancestor of the Douala. They claim to have derived from the Bakota, now situated in northern Gabon, but the major fixed geographic point in their migration towards the north-west is a place called Pitti on the river Dibamba. Later they migrated down the Dibamba to its mouth and northwards to the Wouri river in Cameroon, settling among the Bakoko branch of the Basa. Later the Douala occupied both banks of the Wouri estuary and drove the Basa inland.

The dates for this migration are not clear. Nevertheless, by the beginning of the nineteenth century the Douala are reported as dominating the trade of the Cameroon estuary, under their King Bell, a patrilineal descendant of Ewale. Bell remained paramount chief of the Douala until 1814 when he was partly eclipsed by the head of another section of the tribe, King Akwa. From this time onwards the successors of these chiefs were always known as King Bell and King Akwa; other kings were Dido, Joss and Bonaberi (formerly known as Hickory). The Bells, the Didos, the Akwas and Bonaberis still survive as chiefdoms or family groups.

When the Douala installed themselves in Cameroon around the mouth of the Wouri (the Cameroons River), they began trading with the local Koko and Basa (exchanging fish for Douala agricultural products) and later with the Europeans (ivory and slaves in exchange for cloth, hardware and beads). The Douala inhabited both banks of the Wouri River but the exact dates for their settlement are not clear. The first King Bell, who was a sixth generation descendant of the direct ancestor of the Douala, was reported to be trading with the Europeans in the beginning of the nineteenth century. In his heyday more than twenty-five British vessels were said to have been moored in the river at one time.

The Bakweri claim the same ancestor as the Douala, yet they also claim to have originated from Mboko country via the northern side of the Cameroon mountain. Most of the Bakweri villages in fact claim to have been founded from a group of villages which lie in a belt between 2000 and 3000 feet (660 and 1000 m) up the Cameroon mountain. The expansion has been generally north and south along the mouth, with the largest number going towards the southern and south-eastern foothills.

The tradition of the Buea group, for example, states that a certain Eye Njie used to come from Womboko to hunt on the eastward side of the mountain with a friend, Nakande. Nakande used to hunt near the site of the present Wonakanda, while Eye moved on to a river near the present-day Buea. There he built a hut in which he slept and dried the meat of the animals he killed, which he carried back with him to Womboko after a few days, meeting Nakande on the way. They did this several times and eventually they brought their wives and planted gardens. The settlement became permanent as they were joined by friends and relatives from Womboko. The same story says that the people began to trade with the Douala and the Isuwu from whom they bought gunpowder, cloth and strong drink. Formerly they had bought such things from the Lundu who had obtained them from the Efik of Calabar.

Unlike the Douala chiefs, Bell, Hickory and Akwa, none of the Bakweri people seemed to have obtained wealth and influence through trade with the Europeans along the coast. On the contrary, they seemed to have suffered rather than gained from European commerce and colonisation. Plagued by disease, and a falling birth rate, their lands taken over, their villages swamped by immigrants from the north, the Bakweri have undergone a cultural and demographic crisis from which they are only recently recovering.

Bimbia

The Isuwu of Bimbia also derive from Mboko country. The tribe first came to the notice of history at the time of King Bimbia, although there is some doubt that Bimbia himself was of Isuwu origin. In the 1800s, probably after the time of King Bimbia, the Danes landed some liberated slaves on Nicholl Island, off the coast of the Bimbia promontory, but the islands soon became the resort of fugitive slaves and undesirables. Mention is made at this time of the existence of Europeans and half-castes at a trading establishment at Bimbia. Chief Bile, or King William, was from Bonaberi in Douala, but had moved to Bimbia where his mother's brother lived. During King William's time the Bimbia or Isuwu became an important tribe in the Africa trade of the Cameroon coast, second only to the Douala. In a battle with the Wovea people William had the help of the Acting British Consul, who helped him defeat them and made them recognise him as king of a stretch of mainland and the islands north from Bimbia. It was from King William that Alfred Saker purchased land to found his Baptist mission at Victoria. His successor was murdered by the Bakweri shortly before 1884 on his return by canoe from a trading trip along the coast.

CHAPTER 9

European traders and the Coast

Cameroon had been rediscovered by the Portuguese in the fifteenth century. In 1472 Fernua do Pao discovered the island that bears his name and, presumably, at the same time, caught sight of the coast. Later on, when the Portuguese entered the Wouri estuary (the Cameroons River) they found a variety of prawns swarming in the region, and called the river Rio dos Camarões (River of Prawns). Later, at the time when the New World was divided between the two major European powers, in 1494, Fernando Pô became Spanish and it is the Spanish version of Camarões – Camerones – which gave rise to the Anglicised name of Cameroons.

This is perhaps a convenient place to summarise various versions of this name still used in writings on Cameroon. The German habit was to call the country Kamerun, a German phonetic spelling. The French took this over as Cameroun. The English, more faithful to the original Spanish-Portuguese name, called the country Cameroons. Southern Cameroons and Northern Cameroons were the two regions administered by the British (British Cameroons) under League of Nations mandate and United Nations trusteeship. It is still popularly called the Cameroons, although there seems to be a movement towards following the French spelling of Cameroun. We have tried to be consistent in this book and use Cameroon throughout. It should be noted that Kamerun is still used today, mostly by members of certain political parties – not to imply a return to a German nonemclature, but to refer to the period before Cameroon was divided between the French and the English.

The motives behind Portuguese expansion down the coast of West Africa were fairly straightforward. Apart from a desire to reach the rich eastern Spice Islands by sea, European traders had also been completely excluded from playing a direct part in the rich Saharan trade in gold with the Sudan and forest regions of West Africa. It was only by approaching West Africa by sea that they could hope to open new outlets into the interior which would become a monopoly of sea-faring Europeans and not desert-faring Africans. The Portuguese discoveries in Senegal, Ivory Coast and Ghana in fact effectively destroyed the old caravan routes of the western Sudan. Once the interior of West Africa was thrown open to traders plying the West African coast, the slaves, gold, ivory and ostrich feathers which had been the main exports across the desert could be conveyed to the northern markets by the longer, but safer and cheaper sea route. At the same time European salt carried as ballast in the outgoing vessels began to flood the African markets and this further sapped the trade of the ancient desert highways.

After the exploration of the West African coast in the fifteenth century trading stations were established and by the beginning of the sixteenth century direct trading relations had been opened by sea between West Africa and the newly discovered American continent. No permanent stations were established in Cameroon in the early period, although Cameroonians in thousands were transported across the Atlantic to provide a labour force for the European plantations in America.

Trade

As in the North, slaves had become the most important export commodity of the coast and until the end of the sixteenth century, the Portuguese were the main suppliers, until the Dutch captured Sao Thomé and established a trading post at the mouth of the Rio dos Camarões, thereby breaking the hold of the Portuguese. Then came French, English, Swedish, Danish Brandenburger traders in search of slaves.

The whole coast between the Gold Coast and the Niger Delta was soon known as the Slave Coast. In the seventeenth century because of the rapid growth of the demand for labour by the European plantations in tropical America, plus the growing demand for sugar, the transatlantic slave trade began to dominate European activities in West Africa at the expense of the old trade in spices, pepper, ivory, gold, etc. An estimated 900,000 Negro slaves were landed in America by 1600 and the seventeenth century figure is as high as two and three quarter million; those for the eighteenth and nineteenth centuries are as much as seven million and four million respectively. At first the Dutch were the more important traders, but by the eighteenth century the English and French were the principal competitors in the international trade, British ships alone carrying more than half the slaves to America. The normal practice was for the European

traders to stay on the coast and buy their slaves from African middlemen, such as the Calabar chiefs or the Bimbia and Douala merchants.
The earliest slaves to be exported were possibly local criminals, but
as the demand increased, people living just in and from the coast
began to use the firearms they had acquired through trade to venture
further into the interior and deliberately encourage the capture of
slaves for export.

One of the most important effects of the coming of the Europeans
to the coast, their demands for slaves and their introduction of firearms, was to direct the trade in central Cameroon towards the coast
and away from the northern desert trade routes. For a long period the
Central Plateau region was given up to slave raiding and certain
groups of people served as reservoirs for these razzias. The result was,
as we have seen, a constant scattering of groups and migrations.
Slaving was infectious: the Bamum, for example, had suffered from
Fulani raids, but having beaten them back they themselves began to
raid nearby peoples. Bamileke markets supplied Calabar, the slaves
passing through Upper Cross River areas. The Bangwa, between
Banyang and Bamileke regions, acted as intermediaries and shuttled
slaves to the Cameroon coast to Bimbia, Douala and the Rio del Rey,
where the Europeans had established trading posts. The Douala and
their cousins, the Bimbia, established special links with the inland
Bakossi and Basossi and perhaps beyond, and slaves, ivory and other
interior trade goods came down from the Central Cameroon, primarily via the Mungo route. After the end of open slave trafficking across
the Atlantic, slavery continued to flourish and captives were used
internally for portering oil and kernels and working the oil palm
plantations near the coast.

Nevertheless, the abolition of the slave trade brought important
changes. The island of Fernando Po was occupied for the purpose of
controlling the shipment of slaves from the Bight of Biafra and Benin;
and the name Man o'War Bay on what is now the coast of Fako is a
reminder of the effort the British made to suppress the slave trade,
since this bay offered a place of shelter for the men-of-war of the
British Navy in their coastal patrols to check the trade in slaves across
the Atlantic. It was in the estuary of the Cameroon River, which was
the most important by reason of its excellent harbour and water connections with the interior, that trade took place on board abandoned
ships, anchored in the river. It was originally by barter; natives bringing the products which the Europeans required and receiving cloth,
trinkets, arms, gunpowder and alcohol in return. The Africans
brought ivory, slaves and later palm oil and palm kernels. Trading

was always accompanied by a deal of discussion ('palavering'); money was hardly known, although *kru* (iron bars) or *manillas* (iron or copper bracelet-shaped objects) were sometimes used. Other substitutes were also used for money in the interior, of course, such as salt, tobacco, brass wire, cloth, cowrie shells, fishhooks and gunpowder.

In Cameroon local chiefs showed their intelligence when they realised that if the Europeans were allowed to build strong forts the control of the trade and even the control of their people would pass out of their hands. For this reason the European traders always operated as individuals and possessed no easily defendable bases in Cameroon. They always remained dependent on the goodwill of the chiefs of the local tribes and duty was paid on the trade. The chiefs erected compounds for the storage of slaves awaiting shipment and received payments in pieces of cloth, iron and copper pans and tools and the usual trade goods of the period.

The towns of the Douala trading chiefs, Hickory Town, Bell Town, George Town, grew in prosperity, as a result of this trade. The following is a description of Akwa town taken from the diary of MacGregor Laird and quoted in *The Cameroonian*, June 1962, Accra, 9.

> We entered the great basin of Cameroon River (Moungo) . . . in the morning we went ashore to visit King Akwa. After viewing his house, which was of two stories with a gallery surrounding it outside, we walked through the town, which in order and beauty far exceeded anything I had yet seen in Africa . . . The principal street is about three quarters of a mile in length, about forty yards wide, perfectly straight, and the houses being of the same plan give a regular and handsome appearance.

Profits were made by the chiefs through the *dash* – a gift which was made to the traders and chiefs on the completion of every business transaction. In Douala the traders used to pay the kings a lump sum each year to trade, called *kumi*. Even under German colonial rule, at least up to 1914, this was paid, and provision for its payment was always made in the annual budget. A system of credit also developed between the visiting traders and Cameroonians. It became the custom to give the local traders large quantities of goods on credit, which were to be paid back later, at a certain date, in ivory, rubber, palm oil or palm kernels.

With the competition between European traders the practice got out of hand. The German trader, Woermann, for example, had given the Douala chiefs so much credit by 1884 that he would have lost considerable sums if either the French or English had occupied the country instead of the Germans. This was one of the potent reasons why the Germans wished for a protectorate, and also why the local chief favoured English protection. This credit system, known as 'trust' was abolished by government decree in 1885, but nevertheless it continued. Even as late as 1914 the problems connected with 'trust' remained unsolved, for European traders were arguing that trade in the interior was impossible because of it.

CHAPTER 10

The scramble for the Cameroon

During the nineteenth century Dutch and Portuguese influence had given way to British and German competition on the coast. Fairly early on, local chiefs of the Douala and Bimbia considered seeking the protection of one or other of the European powers. As far as Britain was concerned there was little interest in assuming further colonial responsibility than they already had in West Africa. For this reason they refused to accept an offer in 1833 from the inhabitants of that part of the mainland which stretched from Bimbia to the Rio del Rey. However, British interests were long-standing, both in their preventing the persistence of slave-trafficking and their encouragement of the new trade in palm oil and wild rubber. For such purposes annexation of territory was thought to be unnecessary and trade which was developed was continued to be carried on through local middlemen on the beaches or from hulks of dismantled ships anchored in the river.

The first permanent English settlement was a mission station started near Douala and subsequently moved to a place near Bimbia. Alfred Saker was a Baptist missionary who, assisted by Negro missionaries from Jamaica, had laboured in Fernando Po among Africans freed from slavery on the mainland by English gunboats and sent to the island for refuge. Spanish Jesuits had been horrified at the presence of Protestants and persuaded the Governor to exile them. Saker moved with his flock to the mainland, purchasing from the King of Bimbia a strip of territory ten miles (16 km) long and five miles (8 km) wide along Ambas Bay, at the foot of Mount Cameroon. The land was cleared of jungle and a school built. The Christians organised their own society and government with the missionary in charge as the *de facto* governor of the little colony of Victoria, aided by a court of justice which enforced law and order by imposing fines and the use of the whip. The actual settlement of Victoria, named after the English queen, was in 1858.

At this time English commercial and missionary interests had so far not persuaded the government to establish a protectorate. Nevertheless, gunboats continued to patrol the waters nearby to prevent ships leaving with their booty of slaves and there was a consul to whom the local missionaries and traders reported. A local court set up between traders and natives at Douala reported serious matters to him. However, traders in the seventies felt the need for a more effective control of the region, for fear, particularly, of the French who were moving along the coast towards the Cameroon from the west and from the south, establishing factories and claiming territory and introducing tariffs, which excluded non-French goods.

In Douala trouble between the local chiefs was causing added difficulties. As early as 1864 King Bell of Douala addressed a letter to Queen Victoria requesting permission to visit England. In 1877 a group of chiefs wrote to the queen offering to surrender their territory to her. In November, 1881, King Bell and King Akwa together addressed a petition to Gladstone asking again for annexation to England. Similar requests were made from Bimbia and Victoria.

One of these petitions sent to the Queen is worth quoting:

Dear Madam,
We your servants have join together and thoughts it better to write you a nice loving letter which will tell you all about our wishes. We wish to have your laws in our towns. We want to have every fashion altered, also we will do according to your Consul's word. Plenty wars here in our country. Plenty murder and idol worshippers, perhaps these lines of our writing will look to you as an idle tale.

We have spoken to the English Consul plenty times about an English government here. We never have answer from you, so we wish to write you ourselves.

When we heard about Calabar River that they have all English laws in their towns, and how they put away all their supersitutions, oh, we shall be very glad to be like Calabar, now. (Le Vine, p. 20, 1964).

Further research seems to cast a shadow of doubt as to whether the so-called petitions by Akwa and Bell were in fact motivated by a genuine desire of these kings to seek British protection. The Nigerian historian, Diké, points out (p. 216, 1956):

much has been made of the strange letters written in 1879 and 1881 addressed to the British government by Kings Aquah and Bell of the Cameroons both of whom offered their territories to the Queen of England. Letters of this type so characteristic of the period were sometimes inspired by British traders and were designed to influence the Foreign Office in London to the merchants' requests. These documents must be read with a great deal of discrimination. What is clear however is that the petty kings of the Cameroons were perhaps unable to distinguish between informal control and outright annexation. The Consuls were Governors in all but name and could with little reluctance get the letters from some of the corrupt chieftains of the coast.

Whatever the facts, Edward Hewett, consul in the years 1879 to 1885, had repeatedly advocated the formal annexation of the coastal region of the Cameroons as far as the Benin River, a demand prompted by considerations of interior trade and by fears of the French.

In 1882 Hewett had been told by the British Government that when he returned to his African post he should visit these native chiefs and give them friendly messages in order to keep them from surrendering their territory to France or Portugal. Hewett was ordered to make a lengthy visit to the coast, to visit the estuary, report to the chiefs and report on the situation. Arriving in Douala, Hewett found conditions disturbed. English trade was suffering and German trade increasing. Hewett tried to settle disputes between the chiefs, the traders and reorganise the defunct court of equity. He then wrote a report covering every aspect of the region.

However, difficulties were met from the start. The major ones were financial. Money was needed for the salaries of the consul and the vice-consul, but it was impossible to get funds either from the government or the traders. With news of fresh French and German activities it was decided in April, 1884, to send Hewett without delay and ships were placed at his disposal. Hewett left England as the future consul of Calabar in order to get the treaties signed. They were printed ready with the date, the place and the signature (or the cross) left to be filled in.

As plans were made for the secret scheme to be put into operation, they learnt of rumours that a German gunboat, the *Möwe*, was going to the Cameroon river. On 20 June that year the German agents of the Woermann firm of Hamburg had received instructions to treat with the natives and tell them Germany wanted to annex their country. The chiefs, in despair at the chaos in their country, said that if the English did not take over they would have to hand it over to the Germans.

Meanwhile, in Bonny, Hewett heard of the arrival of the *Möwe* on 14 July and sailed from the Cameroon. But he arrived too late. King Bell and King Akwa had already made their treaty with Dr. Nachtigal who had come on the *Möwe* with instructions from Bismarck to establish German rule. 'Too-late Hewett' was bitterly disappointed. Nervous of French activities, Hewett had not dreamed that Germany had the vaguest colonial ambitions. Of course 'Too-late Hewett' cannot be blamed: perhaps the blame should be taken by British trading firms who refused to give him the small financial support necessary for the administrative control he wished to set up in West Africa, primarily for the benefit of these very commercial interests.

At all events, by the time Hewett arrived in Douala, Dr. Nachtigal had already arrived by German gun-boat, and the German flag had been hoisted in the territory (14 July 1884).

The Germans

In 1884 there were only a limited number of trading stations at the coast. The main European peoples interested in Africa at this period were the French, British, Portuguese and the Germans. After the unification of Germany, a tremendous drive for colonies started in that country, which felt itself behind in the race for influence and economic interest on the continent of Africa.

The sudden *volte face* of all the European powers concerning colonising West Africa at this time seems difficult to understand in terms of the local situation which had hardly changed. In general it was the struggle for power going on inside Europe itself from 1870 and culminating with the first world war, which produced diplomatic and economic rivalries which were played out outside Europe, particularly in Africa. Until the early eighties it seemed that none of the European leaders had any intention of taking over African territories. However, the activities of missionaries and traders made the country ripe for European intervention and development. Britain, for example, had been content to exert a preponderant influence along the West Coast of Africa, leaving political authority in the hands of the Africans.

This growth of German interest, as well as the entry of Belgium on to the African scene created the situation which led to the actual colonisation of Africa by these European powers. The term 'sphere of influence' was used and the Germans began to occupy parts of the coast which had previously been visited by the French, English and Portuguese. Traders in the parliaments of their respective countries began to raise objections and kept asking their governments to annex territories. The British continually refused to take on responsibilities of this kind; the French, on the other hand, were open to suggestion, although they did not realise to what extent their colonial empire would eventually grow.

The question why Germany decided to enter the 'scramble for Africa' is not to be answered simply. Before 1884 Bismarck's speeches show opposition to colonies; but German traders feared both France and England, the two powers engaged in seizing territory along the coast where German trade was already considerable. Moreover, the Germans needed more markets as industrialisation grew apace. They moved into Africa and began to occupy various countries – Togoland, Tanganyika, South-west Africa and Kamerun, as they called the Cameroon.

In the Cameroon, chiefs owed the Germans large sums of money, and their overthrow by local chiefs might have resulted in their inability to pay their debts. The Germans also feared that if Hewett, the British Consul, were successful in obtaining a protectorate, obstacles would be placed in the way of German commerce. Woermann, speaking in 1884, listed five reasons for the need of a German colony there: increased German trade; English opposition to German traders generally; the need for protecting trade against natives; the fear of the French and their high duties; and the fear of the Congo treaty made by Portugal and England.

The situation now began to worry the other powers, particularly when the King of the Belgians put his personal fortune into African exploration with an eye to expansion in the Congo. A conference was called in Berlin by Emperor Wilhelm I in 1884–5. This conference is very important for the history of Africa; it laid down the rule that if Europeans wanted to claim a territory, that territory had to be actually occupied. As a result the occupation of Africa – the so-called 'scramble for Africa' – now began. It explains the comings and goings, competitive treaties and hesitations of the Germans, French and British who now began to scramble round the coast of Cameroon. It now meant that the influence merchants and missionaries had in Africa, particularly British ones, had no significance unless administrations were established. Thus, once the Germans began to restrict the activities of the British in Cameroon both trader and missionary would have to leave. The British reply was to place the coast between Lagos and the Cameroon under a protectorate – the Oil Rivers Protectorate.

The German Treaties

Nachtigal, who signed the treaties with the Douala chiefs, had been an explorer in the Sudan and German Consul-General in Tunis. Bismarck claimed that he had been sent out to reconnoitre the territory, but that fear of territorial occupation by others led to the broadening of his instructions by authorising him to place the country under the protection of the Emperor of Germany. In many ways Nachtigal was the personal emissary of the two great German commercial houses, Woermann and Jantzen und Thormählen, since he was instructed by the traders to claim for Germany whatever land the two German firms had acquired already or would acquire by treaty in places that they named.

Two documents were signed at the time. The first was an expression of the wishes of the local chiefs, in which it was clear that the Europeans agreed to keep out of the markets in the interior and to continue providing credit facilities to carry on that trade. The chiefs also stipulated that no land should be taken from them. This document was important as far as later developments were concerned. The second document was the treaty between the Germans and the kings. Sovereignty over the land was given to the German traders under certain conditions: rights of third parties to be respected, treaties of commerce and friendship with others were to remain in force, kumi (a gift to natives for the right of trade) was to be paid as in the past, native customs were to be respected and cultivated land was to remain the property of the present owners.

The question of the validity of the final German treaties has been raised. Before the treaty the local chiefs, who preferred English control, had harboured a great deal of hostility against the Germans. To overcome this hostile opinion the Germans resorted to bribery. They also exerted pressure on King Bell who stood in very great debt to the German traders. The question is, did the chiefs of Douala possess the power to sign away their sovereignty in this way? The chiefs had little extensive authority beyond their villages and it is doubtful how far afield the treaties were binding, assuming they had the support of their immediate subjects when they entered into these treaties of 'protection'. Furthermore, it has been asked how far the people of the whole of Cameroon could be bound by decisions taken at the Berlin Conference.

At other places along the coast, treaties were also signed. It was always a difficult business, since no-one knew the extent of the land over which the chiefs had powers; and these chiefs had little knowledge of the meaning of the crosses they put on the treaties. Rum, tobacco, biscuits, trade articles were all used in persuading them. At this time the English were competing with the Germans for signatures and sometimes each got the same cross from the identical chiefs. The situation became unsatisfactory to both English and Germans, and neither country had control of a block of territory. British and German

interests conflicted in other spheres. In Douala the English missionaries protested against German occupation. The English in Douala,
particularly in Hickory Town where the Germans had least authority, were accused of inciting the locals against German rule.
Many rebellions broke out, one resulting in the burning of Bell Town
by the people of Hickory Town. This unsettled state of affairs was
settled when Cameroon was handed over to Germany at the Berlin
Conference and finally boundaries between Cameroon and French
and English territories were settled. The Germans successfully forced
the English to surrender their claims based on treaties made with
chiefs. In any case they were all preliminary treaties due to expire
after six months. The Germans also wanted the English settlement
at Victoria which the missionaries owned by reason of purchase
from the King of Bimbia, along with the islands in Ambas Bay,
while the boundary between English and German interests became
the right bank of the Rio del Rey, still considered to be a river, and
a boundary drawn from the 'rapids' of the Cross River along a line
drawn to Yola.

The following quotation gives an example of the rather casual
way in which boundaries were settled. Sir Clavel MacDonald wrote
about the fixing of the boundary between Nigeria and Cameroon at
Yola (Prescott, J.R.V. 1958):

> In those days we just took a pencil and a ruler and we put it down
> at Old Calabar and drew that line up to Yola. The following year,
> I was sent to Berlin to endeavour to get from the German authorities
> some rectification of the blue line...(and)...my instructions were
> to grab as much as I could. I was provided with the only map...a
> naval chart with all the boundaries of the sea carefully marked on
> ...but the rest was white...except...for a river Akpaoff which
> started near the Calabar River and meandered 800 miles on the
> map. That was to be the boundary...however...there was no
> such river and the only river there was $3\frac{1}{2}$ miles long.

A treaty with the French was concluded on 24 December 1885,
whereby Germany renounced all rights south of the Campo River
and the French surrendered rights north of the boundary, which
followed the Campo River.

CHAPTER 11

The Germans
explore in Cameroon

When the local Douala kings agreed to hand over their sovereignty to the Germans, the Cameroon – or at least a coastal strip – became a German colony. The Baptists at Victoria were replaced by Basel (German-speaking) missionaries and the capital was established at Buea. Almost immediately, the Germans began to regret their promises to the Douala kings that they would not interfere in the interior trade and would leave the trading monopolies to them. In 1884 the territory they occupied was confined to the coast around Douala and Victoria and the control exercised by the Douala middlemen became more and more irksome. The Germans, independently, began to explore the interior in order to see for themselves where the trade goods were coming from and from this time on hostilities with the Douala chiefs became inevitable. The Germans feared their influence inland and even refused to allow the Douala language to be taught in mission schools which were being established in the interior.

Unfortunately, by accepting the document containing the expressed wishes of the Douala chiefs in 1884, the Germans had recognised this monopoly and had promised to refrain from any competition – it had only been by making that promise that they had persuaded the chiefs to accept German, rather than English rule. They felt baulked at being excluded from this trade and attempted to get round it by saying that Douala rights only extended as far as the rapids and that outside this restricted area trade was free to all. All along the coast other tribes had similar monopolies and were determined to fight their European competitor.

Exploration
Consequently, the Germans determined to explore the interior. Not only did they wish to bypass the monopolist Douala traders, but they also feared French and English influence in the north. Moreover, the shortage of labour which resulted after the development of new

plantations meant that fresh sources of labour had to be tapped in the interior regions of Cameroon.

Explorations were first made from the north. The value of Adamawa, the name given to the large region of the Cameroon hinterland lying north and south of the Benue River, had been known to German traders for many years, because of the goods that came from the region and also from reports of the explorers who had been there. In the 1850s Barth had worked in the interior on behalf of the Royal Geographical Society of London. In the sixties Rohlfs and later Gustav Nachtigal had explored those lands and reported on their value, visiting the Kotoko kingdom of Logone-Birni. In 1879 and later in the early 1880s Flegel, a German explorer and trader, had entered Adamawa by way of the Niger and Benue Rivers and was so much impressed by the opportunities for trade that he sought to organise a German trading company for its exploitation.

Exploration from the south was still hindered by the Douala kings. The Doualas' knowledge of the forest routes prevented the Germans making their own way to interior markets and their possession of superior European firearms meant that they could easily prevent the inland Cameroonians from reaching the coast for direct trade with the Europeans. When the Germans learned that much of the trade was being sent through Banyang and Bangwa middlemen towards the English in Nigeria, or even south to the French in the Upper Congo, they made a determined effort to discover overland routes from the coast with the aid of soldiers. First steps were made near the coast. Mount Cameroon was explored and the German flag raised at Buea. Wherever the Germans went they held palavers with the natives, informed them of their new duties as German subjects, settled disputes and recognised the chiefs.

The first German to make significant progress in the opening up of Central Cameroon was Zintgraff, who entered the service of the German Government after a period of exploration in the Congo. In 1886–7, he made some tentative expeditions around the Wouri estuary. In 1888 he travelled by water from Douala, the seat of the Cameroon Government at the time, up the creeks and the Mungo river to Mundame, a Balong village in Meme, where a large factory was set up. He then went on to Kumba and Barombi, which became the first government station in the area, and from there to Nguti and Banyang country, where the Banyang were hostile, reaching Bali in January 1889. He made a blood pact with the Fon. Zintgraff decided to build a station among the friendly and powerful Bali, a people who were also keen to make direct trading contacts with the Germans. He

Zintgraff, the German explorer

then left Bali and travelled north through hostile Bafut into Adamawa. Here is a description, written by Zintgraff, of his encounter
with the Bali chief, Galega (Chilver, 1966, p. 2).

> ...we went a little way uphill and met the first messengers of the
> chief of Bali. These were about twenty warriors armed with spears
> and dane-guns led by three elders clad in shirt-like cloaks. The
> warriors were bare to the waist and wore an apron-like loin-cloth.
> The spokesman, as envoy of the chief, carried a bundle of spears;
> the spearheads were covered in sheaths of black goatskin, decorated
> with leather bands, as a symbol of peace....
> Before us, gently rising, lay a large open square, lined on two
> sides with huts, into which numerous lanes led from different
> directions. In front of us was the extensive compound of the chief,
> hidden by finely woven mat walls and overhung by shady trees.
> Before it, not far from a gate to the right, there arose, in the square
> itself, a large assembly house open on two sides. On the upper side
> of the square squatted about 2,000 warriors, their dane-guns and

spears upright between knees, in perfect silence...

Finally the chief appeared... A big, well-fleshed figure, wearing a dark-red burnous whose ample folds increased his massiveness, he stood upright before his stone seat and looked at me keenly... then suddenly seized my right wrist and raised my arm, and told his fifty or so elders that the white man's skin did not burn, as he had been told, and that he could not possibly have come up out of the water. Then he looked closely at my hand and fingers and seemed satisfied with his inspection. Then he sat beside me... while a servant came with heated palm wine, dividing a kola nut he gave me one half and ate the other. Then he had my cup filled with wine, and after pouring a little on the earth, drank some and passed the cup to me.

On his return to the coast Zintgraff met a degree of hostility from the Banyang peoples, partly because the Bali people he was travelling with upset many Grassfields people who were settled in the Banyang slave villages, but also because a Banyang princess, the daughter of Difang, had died in mysterious circumstances and Zintgraff had been blamed for bewitching her.

Zintgraff did more than anyone else to open Cameroon to German trade and administration. After his first journey, he returned to Germany and argued that the western Grassfields should be developed for German trade, as a market for German exports and as a recruiting area for soldiers and labourers. His real aim was to unite the Grassfields under the leadership of the people he knew and liked, the powerful Bali; as a result the government authorised him to lead a new exploring and trading expedition. In fact, on his second expedition the Germans started trading, mainly for ivory, and also made an agreement with Fon Galega I for the supply of plantation labour.

It was during Zintgraff's second trip that serious hostilities with the chiefdom of Bafut occurred. Zintgraff had passed, in April 1889, through Bafut en route to the Benue and became convinced that the chief was hostile to his plan and aimed to capture his booty. Zintgraff, unawares, had commited two breaches of etiquette, and moreover, his plan to open a road to Takum and Adamawa, where slave raids were constantly made, might have been disliked.

At all events, when the Germans tried to start up ivory trading late in 1890, war was the result and, when the chief refused to pay compensation for the killing of Zintgraff's two messengers, Zintgraff with his Bali allies attacked Mankon and then Bafut. In a combined counter-attack, Bafut and Mankon defeated the Germans and the heads of four of Zintgraff's German companions were taken and displayed in Bafut. The Germans and their allies were not avenged

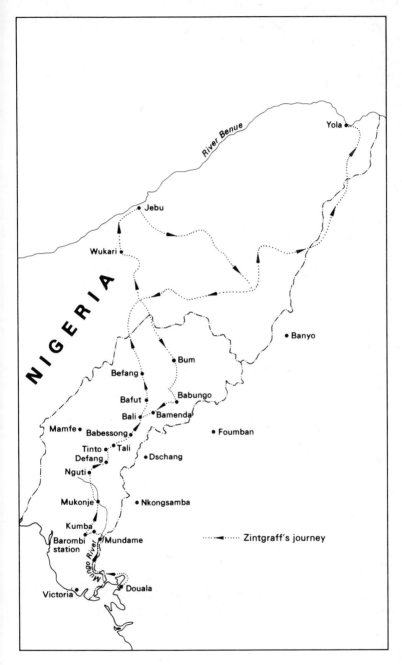

6 Zintgraff's journey

until Pavel's expedition in 1901, when Bafut casualities were heavy and several hundred prisoners were taken as penal labourers. Even so, the chief found it difficult to submit and he suffered further punitive patrols; in 1907 the palace was burnt and the king was persuaded to give himself up, remaining in exile at the coast for over a year.

Zintgraff died in 1897 on his way home to Germany. His achievements were permanent, however, and the route between the coast and Bamenda did not disappear after he and his lieutenants left. Another trader and labour-recruiter, Conrau, was active around Bali and Bamenda until 1899, when he was killed along with his Bali companion on a recruiting tour in Fontem.

In 1895, the link between Bali and the coast was strengthened by the re-establishment of the station at Barombi. The hold of the middlemen in the south was broken and the inland tribes knew that if they came south to the Mundame factory, they could sell their produce for higher prices. One recruiting expedition brought down 640 Bali labourers in April, 1899, and this was followed by other parties bringing the total up to more than a thousand. Bali groups came to Mundame with ivory, wild rubber and animals. They also brought down slaves, mostly acquired from the Bamileke and Bamum and other western grassfields, whom they sold to palm oil traders from Douala and Mbonge, who used them for portering oil and kernels. Profits from the domestic slave trade were good and the Bali traders got in return large quantities of cloth, gunpowder and dane-guns, beads, salt and gin. In 1890, a male slave fetched thirty bales of striped, or dark blue, cloth at Kumba. Women were valued more highly.

During the period that Bamenda and what is now Manyu were being pacified, other explorers reached Yaounde and erected a station twenty-two days' journey from the coast. This became an important German town, a centre of trade, a bulwark against Islam, and a point of departure for expeditions to the interior. Ibi on the Benue was reached from Yaounde and Ngila, Yoko, Tibati and Banyo were visited on the way. Steps were then made to establish claims in the eastern hinterland of the Cameroon; this was the beginning of the 'race for Chad' in which the competitors were France, England and Germany. Finally the treaty, which gave the country her form and size as Kamerun, was signed in March 1894; now the Germans were free to explore the interior and establish German administration throughout their new colony.

Both the German government and the Colonial Society (see p. 80) were active in the north in the late 1890s. In 1899 Kamptz finally captured the Fulani city of Tibati whose lamido was one of the numerous vassals of the emir of Yola. In 1901, garrisons were placed in Garoua and Maroua. Boundaries were settled. The French were even persuaded to retire from the capital of Rabeh's empire, Dikwa, which now came within the boundary of Cameroon. Puttkamer, the Governor, visited the Upper Benue and arranged for the provision of the territory. The Fulani prince at Garoua had no feeling of obligation or loyalty to the new Yola emir, since he was but a puppet successor to the one driven out by the English in 1901. It was considered necessary to rule in Adamawa through the Islamic emirs.

Instead of organising garrisons and posts the Germans retained the Fulani organisation and ruled through it. Under Fulani and Hausa rulers lived the original inhabitants of the land who had been reduced to a form of serfdom, although many independent tribes had sought refuge in the mountains. In this part of Adamawa, under Fulani control, there were large trading centres from which radiated roads, followed by the Hausa trading caravans to and from regions, rich in rubber, gutta-percha and kolanuts. Yola, which was under the English, was a city of over 30,000 people, while Banyo and Ngaoundere had 10,000 and 20,000 respectively. These towns were defended by walls and ditches as a protection against the enemy which might have defeated their mounted soldiery.

The administrative system of the Fulani struck the Germans as being in complete contrast with the 'anarchy' of village government in the south. It was well organised, unified and the lamidos exercised extensive control in their quasi-feudal system. The German advisers were restricted in their role, the sixty or so local rulers, on the whole, being left to administer the region themselves. Their officials even collected taxes, the chiefs receiving a percentage of the amounts collected. Chiefs adjudicated disputes according to native law. It was really the same system developed by Britain in their West African colonies which became known as indirect rule.

CHAPTER 12

Wars against the Germans

Throughout the early period of German exploration and commercial penetration, fighting between the Europeans and Cameroonians was almost continuous in some part of the country or other. Scarcely a year went past after 1888 without open hostilities in some part of the colony, even though some of the engagements were only of minor importance. In the majority of the cases native interference with the Europeans' trade seemed to have been the chief cause. Traders were constantly asking the government for protection against hostile natives: hostile, often because of the depredations of these very traders and their carriers, who raided their villages for food, or attacked local women.

In fighting with the Cameroonians, the Europeans were usually victorious, however, having far superior weapons. Natives could not accomplish much with spears, poisoned arrows, knives, primitive fortifications and pointed and poisoned sticks stuck in the ground to pierce the feet of soldiers. The modern rifle was kept out of the hands of the Africans, particularly after the unpleasant experience in the early nineties, when Germans were defeated by Cameroonians using guns supplied by Zintgraff. As at Bafut, natives did win one or two victories, but they were temporary, for there was no way of holding out long against the rifle, artillery and machine-gun.

The Germans inflicted harsh terms on defeated tribes, who were obliged to supply labourers to construct roads and railways, to provide protection for missionaries and traders, to pay large indemnities in ivory and other goods and to submit to German authority. In 1904 there was a rising in Mamfe (present-day Manyu), in the north and west–the wars are locally known as 'the Mpawmanku wars'. The insurrection occurred among a group of Keyaka. Anyang, Basho and Manta villages and resulted in the destruction of the German station, leaving houses ruined and towns almost deserted. Graf von Puckler Limburg, the officer in charge of the Mamfe district, was murdered and the station was overrun and looted by local peoples antagonistic to the Germans.

This rising of the Anyang was blamed on Calabar traders whose middleman monopoly had been broken by the new route which had been opened to the coast. It was after this insurrection that the Germans decided that the Banyang, who formerly lived in scattered lineage settlements, should build in more compact village units. Agborkem, which was the original headquarters of the Germans on the Cross River, was transferred near to the present site of Mamfe in 1909, and was named Ossidinge. Between 1907 and 1908, another German officer, Glauning, was killed while attempting to establish German influence in the 'Munshi' areas bordering Nigeria.

On the departure of much of the garrison, many peoples in the Grassfields tried to assert their independence and refused to obey the station; it took six months to restore the situation. The Bali were always calm and obedient and helped the Germans crush resurgents. They were rewarded by being given subject villages. Later the German dependence on the Bali lessened, mainly as they began to fear the influence of this chiefdom, whom they had themselves armed with efficient breechloaders. Bali sub-chiefs were even allowed to collect their own taxes. Fonyonga remained titular overlord of most of the thirty villages under his control, but since the collection of tax was no longer his role, the subsidiary chieftains now regarded themselves as released from all obligations. This destroyed at once the support of the powerful Bali chiefdom.

Many of the rebellions which occurred among inland tribes resulted from the maltreatment meted out to plantation workers, their deaths in the malarial southern zones and the general refusal of most Cameroonians to work willingly in the plantations. In Bangwa, a German agent, Conrau, had recruited eighty-eight men as labourers in the southern plantations, with the consent of his blood-brother, the Fontem chief, Asunganyi. A large number of these Bangwa, coming as they did from outside the malarial zone, died and Asunganyi held the German officer responsible for the disappearance of his subjects. Conrau was imprisoned in Fontem for a period during 1898, finally losing his life trying to escape. The chief fled from the Germans but was captured and sent into exile at Garoua. A station was set up at 'Fontemdorf' and one of the chief's sons, more amenable to the Germans, ruled in his stead.

Retaliation after these revolts was fearful. In November 1901, Pavel started his march from Tinto to Banyo to consolidate the effect of an earlier 1899 expedition to Adamawa and also to punish the

Bangwa, the Mankon and the Bafut in preparation for the establishment of a military station in the Grassfields. Welcomed by the Bali and reinforced by Bali soldiers, Bafut was laid waste despite strong resistance. In the fighting sixty-two Bafut and 218 Mankon were killed, many prisoners taken and some labourers levied.

Towards the east hostilities broke out sporadically and traders always sought protection before entering any unknown or unoccupied area. Fighting among the Bulu (Fang) lasted off and on for three years and rebellions had to be quashed among the Bassa, Bakoko, Kaka and other peoples. The Bakoko, for example, on the road to Yaounde, rose in defence of their trade monopoly and succeeded in cutting off all communications between the station and the coast for a long period.

Conflict in the south was almost endemic. The Bakweri, who occupied the slope of Mount Cameroon began to give trouble early on. In 1891, the Germans had sent an expedition against Gbea (Buea). The story is that two women had been accused of witchcraft after the death of a man, and had been subjected to the sasswood poison ordeal. When they did not vomit the poison mixture, they were considered guilty by the people and hanged. This matter was reported to the Germans by an African Basel Mission preacher, and Gravenreuth and his Dahomean soldiers attacked the Bakweri. The German leader was killed and during the encounter the Bakweri chief Kuva Likenye fled, dying soon afterwards.

His brother and successor, Endeli, escaped to Mokunda among the Lower Bakweri, but was later captured by the Germans and exiled to Douala until the Gbea people had paid their indemnity. This battle took place on December 1891 in a ravine which adjoins the present roundabout and the road to the Mountain Hotel in Buea. After the encounter the Germans retreated to the coast via Bibundi, after burning the town, carrying the head and heart of Gravenreuth with them.

Buea was finally occupied in 1894, when von Stetten and Dominik stormed the town by surprise and brought the inhabitants under German rule. The Bakweri were then moved to their present site and their labour was used in building the government station which was established on the site of the former native village. It was called Buea and became the capital of the Cameroon.

The Germans' biggest headache had always been the Douala, who were basically their commercial rivals. In 1892, a Bali troop brought down to Douala was set upon by the Douala among whom the hated 'German' troops were quartered. The Douala also refused to pay taxes imposed by the Germans, claiming that the 1884 treaty gave them no such rights. The Germans disliked the Douala for other reasons – they refused to work on the new plantations and they refused outright to carry goods for white traders. The final blow for the Douala people came when the Germans declared their firm intention of expropriating Douala land around the estuary and re-selling the land at higher prices to whites.

In 1910, it was decided, in order to prevent land speculation and also to improve health conditions for Europeans, to move the natives from the town to a new location separated from the Europeans by a kilometre. By this act of expropriation, the Douala people were to lose their land and the German Government was to become the owner. Douala was the terminus for the country's railroads and the best harbour; it had had rather a boom and it was even said that Douala might become the capital instead of Buea. As the demand increased, the Douala owners naturally asked for the maximum sums in return for property sold.

Preparations were made for the expropriation in 1911 and the Douala, feeling this was the last straw, refused to submit. The Germans had already ousted them from their monopoly of trade despite official promises of non-interference, and for years they had been objecting to the taxes they were forced to pay. In their violent protests to the plan, the Douala chose as their representative their king, Manga Bell, who proved a very able leader in the fight against the German administration. The Douala people were, in fact, in the right, the expropriation being contrary to the 1884 treaty, and they were supported by many Europeans.

When the administration refused to listen, the Douala people reacted violently. Manga Bell said that this high-handed expropriation of native land was contrary to the treaty of 1884 and he sent a formal telegram of complaint to the Reichstag in Berlin. Nevertheless in 1912, the Douala were moved to their new settlements. Manga Bell, because of his insistent protests, was removed from his post in the administration. His activities led to the sending of a representative to Berlin and he also sought support in the interior of Cameroon – an agent was sent to King Njoya of Bamum with a request for support. Manga Bell was arrested on the charge of treason. He admitted that he tried to contact foreign powers for support in his efforts to keep his people from losing their lands, and was executed as a result.

CHAPTER 13

Missionaries in the Cameroon

Baptists

When the Germans occupied the Cameroon, there were three English Baptist missionary stations in the colony: one at Victoria, and two on the Cameroons River – at Bell Town in Douala and at Hickory across the river. The latter was destroyed during the December 1884 rising. After long negotiations the English missionaries withdrew, mostly to the Congo, where they had opened new missions. In December 1886, the Basel Mission took over the work and property of the English society, although disputes over the price to be paid for the land continued for many years. Relations between Baptist Christians and the German Lutherans were not always good, as the former continued their denominational practices. In many ways the Germans thought the English had given the natives too much independence and self-government in their religious organisation.

In 1889–90, there came a break, the Baptists separating from the Basel group, the Baptist church continuing with African pastors. They carried out missionary work and education to such an extent that the Basel Mission became jealous of the activities of this so-called 'pro-English faction'. They even suspected the Baptists of being the beginning of an independence movement.

Presbyterians

In 1871, the American Presbyterians had a mission in Gabon, and gradually spread their activities towards the north and entered present-day Cameroon between Campo and the Nyong River in east Cameroon. In 1879, the first American missionaries disembarked at Batanga. When the Americans were forced to evacuate their missions in Gabon, the Presbyterians intensified their activities in south-western Cameroon, and began to proselytise in Bulu country. One of the pioneers of the American Presbyterian Missions was the Rev. J. Leighton Wilson.

After 1892, the Americans extended their activities into the interior. In 1897, a hospital was begun at Elat. In 1897 too, they founded a station at Lolodorf. In the war that originated in the desire of the Bulus to defend their trade monopoly (1898–1901), the Presbyterians played an important role as peace-makers. Despite the obstacles put in the way by the German administrators, by 1913, with fifty-six missionaries, the Americans had almost 3000 communicants and almost 10,000 pupils in their schools.

Catholics

In 1884, the Catholic Polish explorer Rogozinski offered the Catholic fathers in Gabon a concession at Bota, not far from the Baptist missionaries, in order to start a Catholic mission. However, this was a period of some political confusion; since the Germans had established their protectorate over Douala in the same year, the Bishop of Libreville did not consider it an opportune time to take up the offer of the Polish explorer. However, in 1885, Admiral Knorr and Dr Nachtigal sought a Catholic mission to be established at Douala, but the German Government refused permission because the missionaries were French.

In 1889, German missionaries, known as the Pallotin Fathers, finally established a mission at Marienberg, at the mouth of the Sanaga river. The head of the first Roman Catholic Mission, the Pallotiner Mission in the Cameroon, was Bishop Vieter, who began a mission station in Central Cameroon at Edea, with the support of the trader, Woermann. Woermann desired to have missionaries near this new trading station, which had been assigned to him by the government for a commercial monopoly. The Pallotiner Mission began its work in 1890 with thirteen workers, and by 1913 it had nineteen European missionaries and over 12,000 pupils in its schools.

During the German colonial period the most important mission group was the Basel Mission. It had its headquarters in Switzerland, but the society had established a German branch at Stuttgart to give itself a German character and to attract money for its work. An important factor in the decision of the Basel missionaries to take over the Baptist Mission was the fear that the Catholics, who had been asking permission to send missionaries to the Cameroons, would be allowed to take over otherwise. The Basel missionaries' first act was to forbid the introduction of alcoholic liquor into the land they had bought from the Baptists, at Victoria. They also started building a health station in 1891 near Buea, but were driven out by an insurrection of the Buea people who were convinced that the missionaries were co-operating with invading German troops.

The Basel Mission was aked to establish a missionary post at Bali, which was considered to be part of the Christian barrier to hold back the march of Islam from the north. In November, 1902, three missionaries visited Bali and decided to make the first Basel Mission site there. They were on good terms with the chief and adopted the Bali language to teach and proselytise. The missionaries often acted as peacemakers between the Germans and the local peoples. They incurred the hostility of German traders when the mission took up trading in 1898, partly to finance its missionary work. The mission had only three or four trading stations, but they were successful and showed that trade could work without bribes and liquor; they also paid the people higher prices. The traders even tried to prevent the Basel Mission from getting government grants to teach German to the natives, until it surrendered its trading business in the colony.

In many other ways the Basel missionaries supported Cameroonians against the German administration. They fought to teach the Bamenda peoples in Mungaka and the southern peoples in Douala, against German preferences. They did what they could to protect Cameroonians working in the plantations, and also helped them fight the administrative policies which took their land and forced them into reservations. They pointed out, for example, that local methods of agriculture meant that farmers required far more land than European estimates would warrant. In Germany they presented a report about the Bakweri, in 1903, in which they said that they had lost their land and had been forced to work on the plantations, six days a week and for long hours, so that only on Sunday could they work their own farms and attend markets.

In 1912 the Basel missionaries wished to work among the Muslims, but they met a refusal since the government had adopted a policy of permitting no missionary activity among the Muslims.

CHAPTER 14

Land and labour under the Germans

During the scant twenty years of German Kamerun's existence, the face of the country radically changed. Rubber and oil palm cultivation was developed: coffee, cocoa, banana and tobacco plantations were established. Factories and trading stations were set up in the interior and roads were opened between Yaounde and Kribi, Douala and Yaounde, Victoria and Buea. The most influential men in early Cameroonian history were not missionaries, explorers, soldiers or administrators, but traders.

The most influential of all these was the Hamburg trader, Adolf Woermann. He was president of a firm, bearing his name, which had been working in West Africa since 1849, although it was not until 1868 that its first trading station was opened in the Cameroon. Woermann also owned a shipping line which ran to West Africa from Germany. Increasing trade, plus the fears of British and French imperial ambitions, made Woermann an active person in the steps leading to the German occupation of the Cameroon in 1884. He had urged upon Bismarck, the German Chancellor, the need of protecting trade in the Cameroons, conferred with him about Nachtigal's mission and given instructions for the guidance of German administrators. His agents made treaties with the local chiefs before Nachtigal arrived. One of his factories even became the first seat of the Colonial Government.

Woermann's interest in opening the interior of the Cameroon to trade was very great and it was he who wanted traders given commercial monopolies in clearly-defined regions. With Jantzen und Thormählen, former agents of his in the colony, he was the first to start plantations in Cameroon. He encouraged German Catholic missionaries to settle there and gave land to the Basel missionaries. Woermann was a trader 'working for his own interests, but in a manner that was enlightened for the larger part, a man whose sense of business realism made him feel that self-interest dictated a policy of

Woermann, a German trader

peace and good treatment for the natives'. (Rudin, 1938, p. 162).

The German Colonial Society

A positive German colonial programme was the result of the energies of private persons like Woermann, rather than from government initiative. And most of the organised pressure for colonial development, in the face of government unwillingness and even opposition, came from a private agency, the greatest of all German colonial organisations, known as the Colonial Society or the Deutsche Kolonial Gesellschaft. This organisation was a development from another colonial society which had aided expeditions going into the interior of the Cameroon and furthered commerce. The Colonial Society, founded in 1884, was a propaganda organisation which favoured German imperialism, and sought to win public support for the colonial movement. It encouraged African studies in Germany such as tropical agriculture, exploration, boundary settlement and all questions to do with the colonies. Of course they were primarily interested in the economic exploitation of the colony, this work being combined with propagandist activity to make the colonies better known in Germany.

The concessions

Individual traders, the Colonial Society and, to a lesser extent, the government, wanted interior trade to be tapped. The Germans learnt that there was a rich hinterland of trade being carried on in the north by the Hausas. They sought to divert this trade from flowing northwards and bring it south to the coast, so that they could benefit by it. When, in 1897, the first Hausa caravan arrived at the coast via Yaounde, the Governor suggested the building of the railroad between Kribi and Yaounde. In 1902, a Hausa caravan, with ivory, arrived from Banyo to Victoria after forty-two days' travelling. It was in Yaounde that the Germans eventually tapped this rich trade and this led them into hostility with the Hausas. To encourage trade, two large trading concessions were formed, the Gesellschaft Sud-Kamerun (The South Cameroon Society) and the Gesellschaft Nordwest Kamerun (the North-West Cameroon Society), which were given the obligation of exploring the land, making roads and, in return, receiving great privileges in their charters. This was in 1898–1899. Each one received nearly one fifth of the whole colony and the government was to share in their profits; the demands for shares, both in Germany and abroad (particularly in Belgium) was great.

The South Cameroon Society found rubber and ivory in unheard-of quantities and trading stations grew rapidly with government support. Individual traders hated the company, which acted as though it had been given an exclusive monopoly of the ivory and rubber goods of the Cameroons. As a result of this and other protests to the government, the original huge concessions were cancelled, and the company was given an outright concession in full ownership of a large tract of uninhabited land, rich in rubber, about one-sixth the size of the original concession.

The North-West Cameroon Society had an even less successful history. It also exercised a virtual monopoly in its concessions. However, it met continual difficulties and incurred heavy losses. The government complained that it had not fulfilled the terms of its

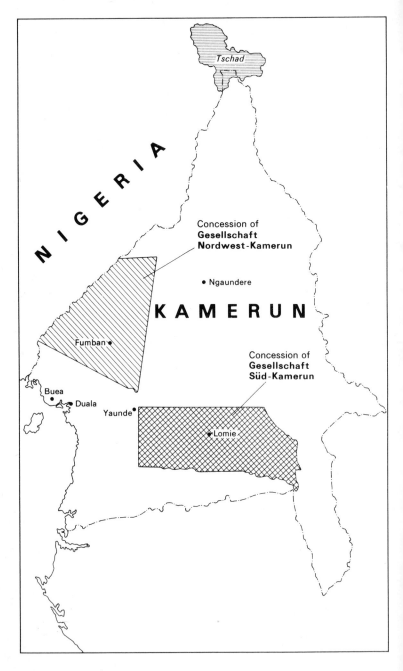

7 German concessions

concession in developing the region, and the concession was abolished in 1910.

Trade and plantations

The economy of the Cameroon is very much an agricultural one, and most developments since the arrival of the Germans were made in the field of agriculture. Perhaps the longest-lasting legacy léft behind by the Germans are the plantations, which still provide the bulk of the income of the peoples in west Cameroon, and have always been a central feature of the economy, in addition to influencing many political situations. At the time of the German occupation, the Cameroon coastal regions were not only sparsely populated but fertile, and this immediately attracted the attention of planters with experience on the Portuguese island of Sao Thomé, which has a similar geological origin. Negotiations were begun with the local people and tracts of largely forest land soon passed into the hands of German planters. Certain circumstances caused the needs of commerce and agriculture to be considered as bedfellows and to be undertaken as joint ventures.

> The most natural one was the hope that the colony would be made to produce commodities like cocoa, tobacco, cotton and the like, which Germany had to import from other countries where their exploitation was known to be profitable. Strong also was the feeling that the commodities obtained from the Cameroons by barter could be improved by plantations, where production and processing would be subject at all points to white and skilled supervision. Rubber, palm oil and palm kernels were gathered by local people in regions where such trees grew wild; their preparation for the trade was according to the crude methods of the natives who cared little about wastage and poor quality. Perhaps of greatest significance was the fact that traders were having increasing difficulty in getting goods from the interior, where fighting and transport costs were serious hazards for all commercial enterprise. (Rudin, 1938, p. 248–249.)

One of the most profitable trade goods was ivory, which in the nineteenth century was in great demand in Europe, used for such things as billiard balls, carvings, piano keys and trimmings for pipes, furniture, etc. At first, Cameroon seemed to have an unlimited supply, but soon this was realised to have been a mistake. Among the traders, competition was very keen for ivory and even government officials joined in this lucrative trade. Fines were paid to the government in ivory at times, and then shipped to Hamburg, where the ivory was sold at auction. Later, the buying of ivory was restricted to certain sized tusks, while the banning of the sale of arms and gunpowder to

Cameroonians also caused a diminishment in the trade.

Palm oil gradually came to be a very important item in exports from the Cameroon to Germany, where it was used for making soap and candles; there were, too, proposals to use it in the making of margarine. In the beginning it came from the interior where trees grew wild, but later the planters turned to the growing of palm trees. In 1903, chiefs in southern Cameroon were required to plant twenty-five palms for each old hut and fifty for each new one. Continued efforts were made by the government to make the local farmers have palm plantations. In 1908 a soap factory was built in Douala.

Cocoa was a successful addition to the Cameroonian economy. When it was planted in Cameroon, it was soon considered in Germany to be of superior quality to the Central and Southern American varieties, and it had no difficulty in finding a market. Since it is a crop that needs a good deal of heat and moisture, the plantations were inevitably found where malaria was present. Some Cameroonians also started their own plantations in the interior.

During German times, rubber was always the most important article of export. The rubber came from latex obtained from extensive wild groves in all parts of the interior, but native methods of extraction were not productive and resulted in the extermination of large areas. Nevertheless it was wild rubber which was exported for the most part. The world crisis in rubber, which arose because of the successful plantations in Sumatra and other places in the Far East, almost killed the Cameroon rubber trade, although it is still grown in the country.

Other crops introduced or developed by the Germans include bananas, initially imported from Costa Rica, tea which was introduced at Tole near Soppo, and the kolanut, which from 1905 began to be grown in plantations in the Cameroon. Other goods, such as timber, ostrich feathers, copal, groundnuts were also exploited, while experiments were carried out in the growth of sugar cane, rice and indigo.

Land

Acquisition of land for the plantations was a problem. When the Germans occupied Douala in 1884, they acquired no land. Land had to be obtained later by purchase or conquest, as for example, in 1885, when the government forced the chiefs to cede land after the 1884 rebellion. Europeans started buying land from locals, often for next to nothing. Then, in 1896, all unoccupied land was declared crown land and commissions were appointed to explore and delimit these 'unoccupied' lands, and transfer of land to Europeans had to have the assent of the Governor. Plantations were developed, with many natives being forced into reservations.

It was the Basel Mission which effected changes in the government's land policy, with the appointment of the first land commission in 1902; this was to look at the land situation, determine the natives' needs and set up boundaries between land held by the local inhabitants and that held by Europeans. Six hectares (15 acres) of land were required for each hut; but all other land was deemed to be unoccupied and hence the property of the government.

Land continued to be alienated to Europeans in large amounts. In 1901, Governor Puttkamer had given to the South Cameroon Society, in full ownership, all unoccupied land in its territorial concessions. As a result the company also regarded all the wild products, rubber in particular, as its property. The government declared that the natives only owned the land they cultivated, yet, in fact, there was land used for goats and cattle, for hunting, or even left lying fallow prior to cultivation in some years' time. In some cases, villages were moved into reservations, of a size large enough to ensure them adequate land for their ends. However, the scheme was inhumane and impractical and natives ran back to the bush, often to find that occupied by the expanding plantations.

How land was acquired

The indigenous system of communally held land took no account of tracts of forest between the scattered homesteads, and there is no doubt, at least at first, that the local chiefs saw little reason for not accepting money for land far from the villages. Most of the title to ownership was by occupation, which the German Government acknowledged when the question of title was raised in 1887. Governor Soden purchased from the natives of Buea all land in Buea not built on or cultivated. Again, various individuals purchased from the government large tracts of crown land of about 2000 to 3000 hectares (5000 to 7500 acres) at an average price of five German marks per hectare. In one case the government actually created crown land to make the transaction possible.

These properties and interest were later amalgamated and merged into the Westafrikanische Pflanzungsgesellschaft, Victoria, usually known as WAPV, the most important of the plantation companies with headquarters at Bota.

The WAPV, Bibundi, purchased their tract of land along the whole of the Bambuko coast from native chiefs with a clause to the effect that ownership should remain vested in the natives. Later, the German Government vested freehold ownership in the company. In another case, four individuals formed a company, acquired land privately and registered it in the government land register (*Grundbuch*). Later it was found that no real purchase existed, but the German Government recognised their title.

Not surprisingly, several problems arose both from the way land was acquired and in the way the land so acquired was put to use. It should be noted that European ideas of land tenure and land alienation are quite different from those of the African. In Africa land is either owned by individuals, groups, communities or villages and it is not necessary to have a clear title to the land. Land was sold to Europeans at rock-bottom prices. It was not thought that the land would be required for use in the present or for use by future generations. It was difficult, however, to explain the meaning to a European of ownership of land. It was only when a Cameroonian sought firewood in the land he had 'sold', or tried to till it, or found his goats and other animals gone that he learned the white man had different ideas from his about ownership.

Plantations

Plantations were established on the lands of the Mboko and Bakweri to the south-east, south and west of the Cameroon Mountain. Alienation of land for this purpose began under the Germans soon after the establishment of a protectorate, in the neighbourhood of the Bimbia and along the Mboko coast, by the Woermann and Jantzen und Thormählen companies. By 1896 almost all the land of the Lower Bakweri and the coastal Mboko had been alienated. This was later rectified to a certain extent and reserves were created for the native inhabitants, which have been further enlarged at various times since, under both the German and British administrations.

Plantation labour

At the time the plantations were opened, the Germans came as managers and technicians and most of them were traders, while they relied for labour on Africans. It was found that the supply of labour from local sources was inadequate. The first labourers on the plantations were from the Bakweri, Bamboko and Isuwu tribes, but it must be added that Bakweri men did not take kindly to agriculture and even if they had been prolific in numbers, very few would have turned up to work except as technicians, clerks, artisans and drivers.

The supply of labour from the Bakweri and other local tribes, became insufficient for the needs of the plantations and a large number of workers from the Cameroons hinterland were imported. This created a problem which has not yet been resolved: the drain of Bakweri women to the plantations and immigrant centres. Since that time these tribes began to decline in numbers, particularly the Isuwu or Bimbia. (This situation has taken a considerable turn for the better in recent years).

The problem of labour was a serious one from the beginning of the German occupation of the Cameroon, and particularly from the moment plantations were established, roads and railways built. Throughout the German period, and indeed right through the mandate and trusteeship periods, goods in most parts of the country were carried by human beings. An example of the extent of this problem is the fact that on the road from Kribi to Yaounde, about 85,000 carriers (men, women and children) were employed at one time; and this figure omits the slaves who carried the Hausas' goods and the wives and children who carried for their husbands and fathers. The feeding and looking after such large numbers of carriers presented a serious problem, and often, when villages were raided for food, fighting resulted in this land of small populations. Horses, oxen and donkeys could not be used because of the tsetse fly.

Workers were also needed for the clearing of the bush for roads, rail-roads and settlements and for working the plantations. There was always a shortage of workers and competition grew up between traders who wanted carriers, and planters who wanted labourers to work their rubber and oil plantations. By 1913, the plantations were employing up to 18,000 native labourers. To get people to work for them, traders and planters, and the government as well, used crude means. They offered liquor, arms and gunpowder to their chiefs with some success. Before the interior was opened, they came from all the European colonies on the west coast from Senegal down to the Congo.

This, however, was hindered by other colonial governments who forbade the shipment of workers from their own colonies for fear that they would not have enough manpower for their own needs. Then, as we have seen, the interior was opened up. The government was asked to get workers from the interior and have them sign contracts for a three or five year period. All kinds of tactics were used to get labourers. Work came to be a penalty imposed on those serving jail sentences; work was the punishment for Cameroonians who made war against the Germans in the interior. Numerous peace treaties with defeated peoples required a pledge from the defeated chiefs to provide workers, sometimes counted in hundreds. Often a tribe would be required to do a specific job of work, such as build a road.

The institution of taxation was the most successful means of forcing men out from their villages to work, since the only means for most of them to find the money to pay the tax was by selling their labour. Those who did not pay tax were given to private employers as labourers in return for paying the delinquents' taxes. In the interior, Bali, Foumban and Yaounde became centres which supplied labour to the plantations. Explorers or plantation representatives made contracts with the chiefs for the supply of workers in specific numbers and specific periods. This system led to many abuses, since contracts were usually signed by the chief, who, more often than not, was unaware of the full implications of the contract.

The recruitment of labour for the plantations built up the Cameroon's economy, but led to many deaths among labourers unused to the climate, diet and conditions of the coast, and often exhausted them by their journey. Epidemics flourished in crowded and insanitary quarters among ill-nourished men. The terrible death-rate among plantation workers, in the early years, made government intervention necessary. Most of the workers came down from the high plateau, the healthy lands of the Grassfields, and worked upon the fertile, humid, malarial lands near the coast. On the whole six months was the maximum period, after which ill-health – or death – meant they had to give up. Many died on the journey to the plantations from disease and – it is said – from nostalgia for their homes and families. The lack of proper food and shelter also played its part. Moreover, the workers were housed in barracks, members of strange, even enemy, tribes being housed together without even a common language to help communication.

Figures for this period are difficult to find out. Early estimates (1901) were that the death rate was 30–50%. Exact figures for the very best plantations were put at 7%; certainly in the case of plantations employing two or three thousand workers the deaths must have been terrible. The high death rate of the early years, of course, lessened as improvements were made.

Workers were not paid in full until their contracts expired, which to a certain extent kept them from running away. It was also supposed that with the accumulated money, the workers would buy goods from plantation 'factories' and return home to the envy of their fellows, thus inspiring the latter to volunteer for work on the plantations and become equally rich in European goods.

The whole problem of plantations, labour, carrying goods, was part of a very general one involving the whole organisation of society. With the development of the interior the social organisation of many tribes suffered indescribable damage. Family life was impossible with husbands, wives and children engaged in carrying, and thousands of men away at the plantations. The health of the whole population also suffered, and not only from the unaccustomed diseases and nostalgia in the plantations; smallpox and other epidemics spread throughout the country and are remembered to this day with dread. Venereal diseases were also spread by carriers. The introduction of hard liquor had its corrupting effects, some carriers taking all their wages in rum. Farms, local trading, crafts became neglected. Villages on the carrying routes were prey to constant attack from hungry, sometimes starving carriers, for whom no provision had been made. Attacks were also made on local women.

CHAPTER 15

German administration

At the head of the administration was the Governor, whose powers were delegated from the German Emperor. He issued decrees, was the highest court of appeal in the Cameroon, headed the military forces and controlled state property. He conferred part of his powers on local administrators, heads of expeditions, of stations or of large administrative districts.

During the thirty years of German rule there were only six governors: Soden (1885–91), Zimmerer (1891–95), Puttkamer (1895–1907); Seitz (1907–10), Gleim (1910–12) and Ebermaier (1912–15). It was under Zimmerer that the most serious scandal of the colony's history occurred, when his chancellor Leist's immorality and cruelty led to violent discontent among the Dahomean soldiery. Under Puttkamer, despite conflicts with the missionaries, his hard policies with the Africans, stories of immorality and the final scandal which ended his office, the Cameroon developed greatly.

In the eighties, administration was confined to the coast and a few nearby settlements; Douala and Victoria were the important centres. When the interior was opened, explorers made treaties with natives and gave the chiefs a flag or some symbol of German authority. Later stations with garrisons of troops were set up at critical points as protection against the almost inevitable attacks on the trade of the Europeans. Rio del Rey and Campo were founded to put an end to smuggling near the northern and southern boundaries. Edea became a station because of Woermann's trading activities. Yaounde was the first interior station, since it was a convenient centre for getting to the north and an entrepot for interior trade. In 1905, it became the head of an administrative district (*Bezirk*). Telegraphic stations (Tinto Wire, Atebong Wire) were established – a network of communications which was not maintained in the British era. The Germans provided harbour facilities in Douala, Kribi, Campo, Tiko and Victoria. These harbours were necessary for the importation of goods into the country and the exportation of raw material from the country to other countries.

The German also opened up railways in the country. Work on the first line of the Cameroons railways was started in 1906. On 1 April 1911, the first 160 kilometres of the northern line, then called 'Manengomba', were opened to traffic between Bonaberi and Nkong-samba. In 1909, construction began on a railway connecting Douala and Yaounde. The intention was to link up with Tanganyika by railway, but the idea was abandoned. Narrow gauge railways were also provided in the plantations to facilitate the transportation of personnel and evacuation of plantation produce.

Once the country had been more or less pacified, German administration fast became intensive. Large administrative districts, or Bezirke, were established in the south, and although stations with garrisons of troops were maintained at critical points, military rule slowly gave way to civil rule and the police replaced the soldiers of the garrisons. Bamenda station was built in 1902 in succession to the one established at Bali by Zintgraff which was abandoned in 1890. Kumba (now Meme) Division was administered from the German centres of Rio del Rey and Barombi, known as Johannsbrechtshohe, founded in 1890. Barombi was mainly established to supervise the trade routes southwest to Mundame. The administrative posts which were open all over the country performed judicial and administrative functions in addition to carrying out missionary and commercial activities.

An advisory council was set up to assist the Governor, with trading firms and missionaries represented. Courts for the Europeans and courts for the Africans were set up. In the latter, whipping, not imprisonment, was the common penalty. The number of Cameroonians punished for violating the law grew from 773 in 1900 to 11,000 in 1912.

A degree of indirect rule was permitted. Chiefs were used to run the two lower courts, appeal to the European administration only coming in the third court. Chieftains also collected taxes. Otherwise Cameroonians were used only in minor capacities, as police soldiers, couriers, mail carriers, interpreters, teachers in government schools, secretaries, river pilots and the like.

Taxation

In 1903 a head tax was proposed for Douala alone, with special payments for plural wives, and this led to violent opposition from the Douala. In 1908 there was the first general tax decree: every grown male capable of labour was obliged to pay six marks a year or perform tax work of thirty days on public works. The sum was raised in 1913 to ten marks. Chiefs helped the government and could get 10% profit. Those who did not pay could be handed over to private employers who would pay their tax. Taxes were also paid for permission to move from place to place for purposes of trade. In the north, the usual direct tax on natives was not in force. The local princes paid tribute to the Cameroon treasury, as they had formerly paid to their overlord at Yola. This tribute, which amounted to 30,000 marks in 1905, was three million marks in 1914.

German achievements included a Botanical Garden, which was opened at Victoria, and a farm and dairy at Buea, where butter, milk, eggs, meat and vegetables could be obtained. There were also experiments in the cross-breeding of cattle. The German traders opened shops or 'factories' in parts of the country, and this afforded an opportunity of selling raw materials and buying imported goods. They built houses in administrative centres such as Buea, Victoria, Douala, Yaounde and Bamenda – some of these are still the best houses one can find in parts of the country today. The most imposing was Government House in Buea, the residence of the Governor of the Cameroon. Migeod remarked:

> More money was expended on the building and the grounds than the German authorities intended. The upstairs accommodation is not extensive and is commonly reputed to be so by design, so that not too many visitors from the Fatherland could be put up.

Education

The Germans opened up schools in the country. The first teacher to be sent from Germany was Christaller who opened a school in Douala in 1888. A second German school was opened in Deido (Douala) in 1890 and a few years later a school was opened in Victoria. The Germans put the Douala and Bali languages into writing although they subsequently realised that the teaching of Douala in schools would spread the influence of their enemies. The educational system placed emphasis on a knowledge of the German language. Funds were given to the missions to open up schools, and in 1913, the missions had 631 schools and a school population of 40,000 pupils.

An Agricultural School was opened in Victoria in 1910 and other schools were opened at Dschang and Yaounde. Natives were trained in the stations, in the interior, in processing palm products and in the preparation of rubber for the market. At Buea there were schools in cabinet-making and upholstering; and a large number of journeymen manufactured furniture, canes, ornamental boxes inlaid with ivory and other objects.

When the British took over the administration of the Cameroons, they found suitable men who had passed through the crucible of German education. These included Steane, Dibonge, Bebe, Ilongo, Cumber, Mokeba and Burnley.

Although German rule in the Cameroon lasted a relatively short time, their achievements were noteworthy. They have been more than favourably compared with the British who made such poor progress in west Cameroon during their forty years of rule. The German colonists were harsh, but they did push the colony forward, invest capital in the country and introduce many advantages from industrial Europe. A Memorandum presented to a visiting United Nations mission in 1949 (Memorandum of the Cameroons Federal Union submitted to the Visiting Mission of the Trusteeship Council of the UNO November 1959 – Zik's Press Limited, Lagos 1949, pp. 14 and 17) gives a clear indication of the attitude of a later generation of Cameroonians to the Germans, particularly in the realm of education where the German system 'was practical' and aimed at making Cameroonians earn a decent living with their heads and hands, whereas British education turned Cameroonians into hewers of wood and drawers of water. During the German regime, there was progress, but at independence workers were still restricted to the plantations begun by Germans or to the lowest ranks of the civil service ladder.

Cameroonians regarded the Germans as being harsh to the point of brutality on occasion, but always just. The brutalities have mostly been forgotten; people remember the Germans in Cameroon for the plantations, the buildings, the railways, the roads and other adjuncts of white civilisation. When the British left the territory, little remained as a heritage of their forty years of rule. Migeod, who visited the British Cameroons in 1923 (just after the British had taken over the government of the territory), remarked:

> On the whole I could not learn that the natives welcomed the change of government. They hoped for great things, and were disappointed. There was trade and prosperity too, in the German days, since much capital was put into the country. Now there is none, and the natives who formerly were well-to-do are now poverty-stricken; and there is not now the means of acquiring wealth. No doubt, trade will improve in time and then the natives will be less down-hearted.

The black record of the Germans is kept alive in the memories of some Cameroonians, not only because of their harsh discipline but because of some accounts of individual personal immorality. Leist, for example, was Acting Governor in 1893. The police force in the Cameroons was manned by soldiers he had brought with him from Dahomey and with whom he had signed a contract that they would work for five years without pay, although the persons they trained and who were less experienced were paid.

> Leist himself made occasional use of the women; once he enter-
> tained guests at dinner by having the Dahomean women perform
> a tribal dance without clothing. After the dance the women were
> distributed to the guests for the night. The women were also
> required to work in government gardens at tasks they did not
> like . . . Leist, angered by the refusal of the Dahomean women to
> work and by their preference for lolling about the streets, ordered
> them to be publicly whipped. They were stripped, placed over bar-
> rels, and then beaten in the presence of soldiers, who were drawn
> up in formation. (Rudin, 1938, p. 211.)

Wehlan, who played a leading part in the suppression of insurrection among the natives, seemed to have taken delight in burning
native villages. Puttkamer, who was Governor of the Cameroon in
1885, was so notorious for his wrong-doings that he was charged in the
Reichstag with conniving at acts of the greatest barbarity committed
by officers of the colonial forces; permitting the mutilation of Africans
killed in action by his soldiers; allowing houses to be built with public
money for himself and for native concubines of officials; keeping at
Government House a German woman whom he called his cousin
and whom he supplied with a passport in an assumed name that she
might return home; and finally, receiving gratuitous shares in several
colonial companies. The result was a reprimand and a fine of £50.

CHAPTER 16

British Cameroons

German rule came to a swift end in 1915, when the circumstances of the first world war meant their defeat at the hands of the French and English. English troops entered Cameroon from Nigeria, aided by Belgian troops from the Congo and French troops from Chad, Ubangi and Gabon. The Germans, of course, were unable to receive any reinforcements and by September 1915, they had to evacuate Douala. Early in the next year the English entered Yaounde. The capitulation of the German garrison at Mora in February 1916 marked the end of the Cameroon campaign and of the German Kamerun Protectorate.

In April 1916 Cameroon was provisionally divided between France and Britain, but boundary adjustments were later made in an agreement signed by Lord Milner and Monsieur Simon on 10 July 1919. After 1915 the British had administered Douala but in 1916 had relinquished it to the French; nevertheless, they had continued to retain, after 1916, the north-west half of the Dschang district, including the town of Dschang, which is part of the Bamileke area of eastern Cameroon. When the Cameroon ceased to become a protectorate and became a mandate of the League of Nations, a body formed after the first world war to maintain future world peace and security, the French and English occupation of the former German territory was confirmed by a division of the country between them. Now the British gave up Dschang to the French and this meant that only twenty thousand Bamileke (the Bangwa) remained in British Cameroons. One reason for the British relinquishing this area to France, and in a sense, breaking the unity of the Grasslands, was the desire not to block the natural hinterland of the Northern Railway which had gone to France.

The division of the country between the two European powers was disproportionate: five-sixths of the territory became a French mandate and the remainder British. For administrative convenience the British-ruled area, British Cameroons, was divided into two parts.

8 The sub-division of British Cameroon

The part contiguous to Northern Nigeria with an area of 17,354 square miles [44,928 sq.km.] was administered as an integral part of three provinces in Northern Nigeria. This part comprised the following: the Tigon-Ndoro-Kentu area, which was administered as part of Benue province; the Southern Adamawa districts, which were administered as part of the Adamawa province; the Northern-Adamawa districts, which were also administered as part of Adamawa province; and Dikwa division, which was administered as part of Bornu province.

The capitals of Benue, Adamawa and Bornu provinces were Maiduguri, Yola and Makurdi respectively and they were all outside the Trust Territory. This part was separated by a gap 45 miles [72 km.] wide near the River Benue.

The southern part of the British part of the country which joined Eastern Nigeria was first to be administered as a province in the southern provinces of Nigeria and later became a province in Eastern Nigeria. The area of this slice was 16,581 square miles [42,928 sq.km.]. Such arrangements were justified, according to a 1919 declaration, by the administrative problem which would have been created by an attempt to constitute these areas into separate and distinct political units.

It will be seen that while the southern part of British Cameroons was wholly a territory by itself, the northern part consisted of parts of three provinces and contained only one administrative unit as large as a division. Moreover, Northern Cameroon was divided by the 45-mile [72 km.] wide gap near the Benue (see map on p. 96). The division of the country into parts, when it was handed over as a whole, resulted from difficulties created by the relief of the territory; differences in the culture of the inhabitants also made it difficult for a sense of national consciousness to develop among the dismembered entities.

France was given an area of 166,800 square miles [431,845 sq.km.] as against Britain's 34,081 square miles [88,036 sq.km.]. The division of the country between France and Britain, in which the people were not consulted, created problems that were to remain the pivotal point in Cameroon politics for more than forty years. The division was not based on any linguistic or ethnic facts but on merely geographical lines – ranges of hills or rivers being arbitrarily considered as natural boundaries. Some ethnic groups, such as the Mbo and Bamileke, were divided, and customs and immigration formalities which were introduced at the frontier made mobility of persons and goods difficult and irritating as will be seen in a subsequent chapter.

The League of Nations

The terms of the mandate were defined by the Council of the League in a document signed on 20 July 1922. The convenant of the League stipulated as follows:

> To those colonies and territories which as a consequence of the late war have ceased to be under the sovereignty of states which formerly governed them, and which are inhabited by peoples not able to stand by themselves, under the strenuous conditions of the modern world, there should be applied the principle that the well-being and development of such peoples form a sacred trust of civilisation.

The mandatary was

> to promote the material and moral well-being and social progress of the inhabitants of the mandated territory and the conduct of the administration was subject to the scrutiny of the League of Nations and its Permanent Mandates Commission in Geneva.

In particular, the mandatary was required to abolish slavery and forced labour, to respect native land rights, and to allow all members of the League free access to, and equal rights in, the territory, while they were forbidden to set up economic monopolies or to develop the territory as a military or naval base. The mandatary could, however, carry out forced labour for essential public works and services, provided that there was adequate remuneration. The natives were to be protected by a careful supervision of labour contracts and the recruiting of labour.

Other duties devolved on the mandatary power – traffic in arms and liquor had to be controlled, for example, and the native laws and customs of the people had to be respected in any form of legislation which should also safeguard native interests.

> The conveyance of land from natives to non-natives is to be controlled, and on commercial matters, equality of treatment is to be accorded to the State members of the League of Nations. Freedom of conscience is to be ensured and missionaries who are nationals of the Members of the League of Nations are at liberty to carry out their work, subject only to necessary control on the part of the mandatory.

The mandatary power had to submit annual reports to the Council of the League of Nations containing information in respect of measures taken to apply the provisions of the mandate. The annual report was written on the basis of a questionnaire prepared by the Permanent Mandates Commission and its charter dealt with public finance, taxation, trade, judicial matters, arms, liquor, etc.

With the division of the country came the parting of the ways in the evolution and history of each sector, which was governed by a European power whose colonial policy was moulded by the circumstances of its history and former experience with colonial peoples.

In fact, the history of the British Cameroons and French Cameroon for the next half-century becomes to a large extent part and parcel of the history of French West Africa and British Nigeria. The activities of the League were restricted in the Cameroons. Despite notable achievements elsewhere in the world it was an organisation doomed to failure. World powers, such as the United States, had never been members; and in important disputes it was powerless or discriminatory. The mere fact of the second world war (3 September, 1939), when Europe was once again plunged into violent conflict, shows beyond a doubt that the League of Nations failed to achieve the purpose for which it was created.

The British Cameroons as a mandated territory

While the eastern mandated unit, known as Cameroun, was incorporated into the French African colonial regime as a separate administrative unit, British Cameroons was treated for administrative purposes as part of Nigeria. Even in the Cameroon the famous Nigerian 'North-South' principle, which had been applied for so long in Nigeria was perpetuated in the division between 'Northern' and 'Southern Cameroons'. The latter, which became West Cameroon at independence remained a separate administrative unit, but the northern mandated territory never had a separate administrative existence, being divided up among several northern Nigerian provinces. Southern Cameroons existed as a separate Nigerian province for more than twenty-five years, until 1949, in fact, when it was temporarily divided into two provinces, the Bamenda and Cameroons Provinces. These were, however, abolished by the new constitutional situation in 1954.

Throughout this inter-war period, therefore, the history of British Cameroons was closely associated with that of Nigeria. Britain did not claim sovereignty over these areas, nor were they colonies. The mandate for the territory had stipulated that Cameroon be administered as an integral part of Nigeria and this was a deliberate act on the part of the British who considered it the only possible way by which the political, social, economic and social advancement of the territories could be assured. It was perhaps the only way that it could be administered at all, since the British Cameroons was a narrow strip of territory and it was also divided into two quite separate areas which

99

were not at all self-contained in a geographical, ethnic or economic sense.

The Northern Cameroons' political development remained entirely separate from that of the south, and our history of political events in the British Cameroons from the 1920s to reunification is concerned primarily with the Southern Cameroons province. The people of the north never participated in the national aspirations of the south, apart from a short period during the United Nations plebiscites. The north was immediately incorporated into the classic pattern of indirect rule, under the traditional emirs of Northern Nigeria. Without even the degree of economic and educational progress which the south experienced, the Northern Cameroons did not develop any political self-consciousness outside their own narrow world.

The British always maintained the wisdom of this course of action. When the United Nations visiting mission visited the British Cameroons in 1949, they gave several reasons why the territory should be administered as part of Nigeria. The territory was sparsely populated, without any tribal or political homogeneity. Tribal boundaries, if they could be defined at all, ran latitudinally – that is, into Nigeria, like the Banyang-Ekoi group – not longitudinally. In many ways, the effect of the new association with Nigeria was to restore historic connections between tribes and states, hitherto divided by the old Anglo-German frontier. Of course, it was soon to be pointed out that while it was true that some tribes had relations in Nigeria, many more had affinities with the inhabitants of the part of Cameroon under French mandate.

Undoubtedly the people of the British Cameroons enjoyed many advantages from the Nigerian connection. Their integration with Nigeria enabled them to share in the political, economic and social advancement of this country. Constitutional advances were made, particularly after the second world war, as a result of the 1953, 1957 and 1958 constitutional conferences. The services of certain experts in Nigeria were automatically available to the British Cameroons in respect of agriculture, forestry, electricity, etc. Facilities, such as the bulk oil plant for the export of palm oil from Calabar, the waterways and harbour facilities of Nigeria, and the Nigerian railways, provided a means for exporting produce which would otherwise have been sent overland. Cameroonians attended schools and colleges in Nigeria and were awarded Nigerian scholarships.

Nevertheless Cameroonian politicians always felt that the British Cameroon was being administered as an appendage of Nigeria and that it did not receive the direct attention of the administering authority as required by its distinct status. It is certain that the Cameroons was in many ways a geographical and administrative backwater and a certain amount of neglect resulted during the mandate period. Until 1949, the seat of government was still in Lagos. And until 1954, when Southern Cameroons was separated from the Eastern Region of Nigeria, there was no separate budget for the territory as government revenues accruing there were included in budgets of Nigeria as a whole and expenditure was allocated, not on the basis of its overall needs, but on the basis of the needs of the various Nigerian regions to which it was administratively integrated.

Between the wars there were few or no political events to be recorded. Disturbances occurred among the Kirdi in the north and there were the occasional border problems between the two mandated territories. On the whole the economic situation was poor in both territories, the slump in world prices during the depression and the reluctance of the British to finance any new undertaking being the prime reasons for this.

There was very little government expenditure, either on the social services or on public works and the economy remained centred on the plantations which the Germans had developed. The territory ran on a deficit throughout the period of the mandate and acquired subsidies from the Nigerian budget, a pattern which was resumed after the second world war.

Inevitably during the inter-war years both African and European interests were more concerned with economic than political problems. The British Cameroons' isolated geographic position – isolated from Nigerian centres of activity as well as from its mandated neighbour, French Cameroon – was the greatest hindrance to economic progress. The Southern Cameroons, for example, was divided into two populous regions, the agricultural plateau lands of the North – Bamenda – and the commercially developed coast with the port of Victoria and the old German capital of Buea. Between these two regions was a forested, hilly, thinly populated region and the problem of establishing communications between the coastal and highland regions has always been a serious one. From the coast, there was a road to Kumba where it was joined by a little-used route from the French Cameroon. It continued from Kumba over a hilly region until it dropped down into Mamfe on the Cross River. (See map on p. 102). In the mandate period, communications to Nigeria during the rainy season were made by way of the Cross River to Calabar. From Mamfe the road runs north-east towards Bamenda, climbing an escarpment from the

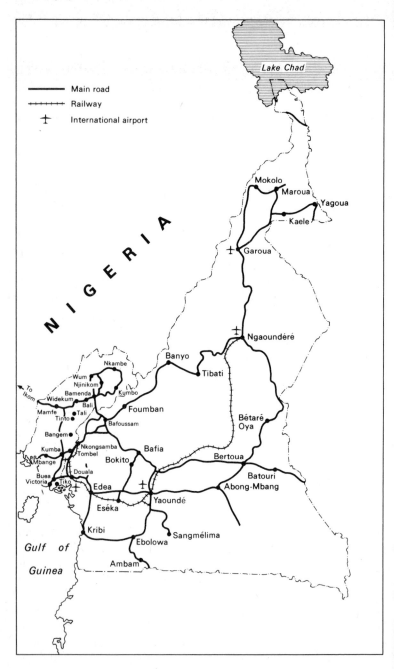

9 Major towns and communications

forest to the plateau; this part was closed in the wet season. Towards the end of the mandate period a 'ring road' joined Bamenda with Nkambe. Bamenda now had a population of about 350,000 and was more populous than Mamfe and Nkambe (present-day Manyu and Donga Divisions), until it was partitioned.

The whole of the Grasslands area with a population of over half a million was left virtually without communications and for months of the year was cut off from the south. There never was any road at all to Northern Cameroons. Large areas throughout Southern Cameroons were isolated from administrative and commercial centres. The commercial centre of the territory was at the coast, with its poor dry season route to the north, had only sea communications with the important centres of Douala and Calabar. Local trading and even interprovincial trading was carried on by head-loading over long distances. Administrative officers often trekked for weeks to arrive at villages under their jurisdiction. As Edwin Ardener pointed out (1967), this isolation remained central to the social, political and economic development of the country.

The plantations

The most important factor in the economic development of the Southern Cameroons before the second world war was the development of the plantations. In 1914–15, when the French and British forces had established control over German Kamerun, the properties of the Germans had been confiscated and handed over to the Custodian of Enemy Property to be administered for the duration of the war. When the British took over the administration of the Cameroons the plantations were merged into a single whole and a government department was formed to administer them. By 1922, however, they had already decided that it would be in the best interests of the Territory and its inhabitants to turn the plantations back into the hands of private – non-African, of course – enterprise.

The possibility of returning the land to the original native owners was considered, but the Lieutenant-Governor of the Southern Provinces of Nigeria maintained that it would have been impracticable to split the plantations into small plots for Cameroonian owners – since without capital backing, the buildings and machinery would fall into ruins. Moreover, he feared that the natives' lack of experience would mean that disease would spread among the crops and the cocoa plants would be destroyed. Consequently in 1922, the Custodian of Enemy Property was directed to sell the estates to anyone except for ex-enemy nationals. When the estates were put up for sale in London in 1923, almost all of them failed to find buyers, possibly due to a lack of certainty as to the security of title. Large amounts of money were needed to put the plantations back into operation and at the time the low level of prices obtaining for raw products must have been a determining factor. Nevertheless in French Cameroon estates were purchased by French, British and Cameroonians.

Another auction was held in London in November 1924 with the restrictions against German nationals withdrawn. All the plantations, apart from small lots, were sold to the original German owners. In 1936, for example, almost 300,000 acres of land were in German hands and less than 20,000 in British. The prices, which included buildings, houses, factories, rolling stock, bridges, wharves and railways, were less than those offered in 1922.

The situation in the British Cameroons after 1924, therefore, was that although the territory was under British rule, there were three times as many German expatriates as British, and the pattern of trade in the territory was not with Britain but with Germany, to which the bulk of the plantation produce was still shipped and from which one half the territory's imports was derived. In 1939 all the estates but one were in the hands of German companies or German individual owners, such as Westafrikanische Pflanzungsgesellschaft, Victoria, the African Fruit Company, Likomba Plantations, Kamerun Kautschukgesellschaft, or individual German owners at places such as Debundscha, Isobi, Idenau, Holtfoth. In 1925, two years after being returned to their owners, the plantations were in full production. Throughout the years preceding the second world war there is no doubt that the plantations flourished, proving in fact to be the main financial and economic support of the territory. The Germans also did much to improve the coastal regions, expanding the port facilities at Tiko and Victoria and constructing shops, warehouses and offices.

An important aspect of the plantations was the number of foreign workers attracted to the Southern Cameroons, from Nigeria and French Cameroon, people who were later to play an important role in political developments in the territory. Large numbers came from the highlands of French Cameroon and their numbers are presumably proof of the advantages to be gained from working in the British Cameroons and the relatively good working conditions. Possibly the French system of forced labour in the construction projects played a part in this situation. Many of these labourers remained as permanent settlers and contributed in a positive manner to the eventual political emancipation of the Southern Cameroons.

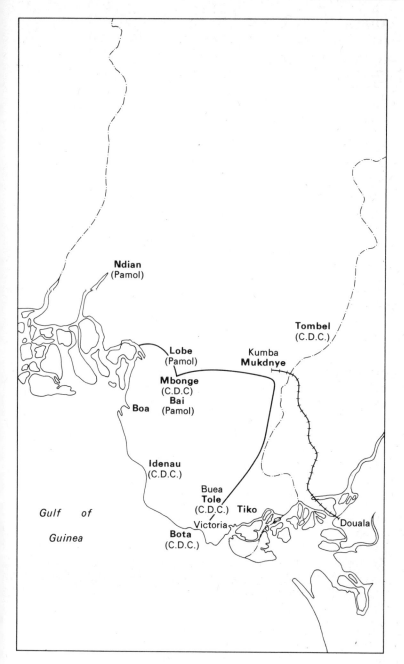

10 Plantations in west Cameroon

Alienation of land

It was during this period that attention began to be drawn to the effects of land alienation on the social and economic life of the people who lived in the areas of the plantations. Even in the 1920s the British were not unaware of the problem facing the natives of Victoria Division, as the following extracts from the 1926 Cameroon Report show.

> There is no doubt that their relegation to reserves has to a large extent made them lose interest in life, as is demonstrated by the dilapidated state of their homes and their neglect of most sanitary measures in spite of years of culture contact with Europeans. Even if the land allotted to them appears large enough for their needs it is invariably not fertile, for the best land has been apportioned to aliens.
>
> Nor is it surprising that interest in life has been lost when they have seen their native organisation and institutions ruthlessly broken up to make way for foreign ideas and enterprise.
>
> While it is not argued that the Bakweri would have cultivated the land in as scientific a manner to such quick profit as it has been by European capitalists there is little doubt that they would have been healthier and happier people if there had been no large alienation of land, but a policy of promoting production by the native himself on his own land, as has been followed with such excellent results in the Gold Coast. The development would have been slower but it would have been surer, as it would have been possible to have maintained the framework of the native system of government and preserved for the people that racial pride and self-respect which have now to a large extent been lost.

Another problem which began to be faced in the coastal regions was the arrival of strangers who settled on land in which they enjoyed usufructuary rights. The Bakweri had a tendency to prefer renting their land or selling it outright rather than working it themselves. Nevertheless when strangers tried to pursue legitimate claims about land against natives there were outbursts of strong resentment. The land shortage which the Bakweri began to feel was due not only to plantations or to the fact that the Bakweri had too little land, but to the number of immigrants who had taken over the use of the land and proved themselves more industrious than the local people. Immigration labour also caused problems for the home areas. The plantations caused people to migrate from north to south, towards Kumba and Victoria where employment opportunities were available. Mamfe, in particular, began to be affected by rural depopulation. One effect was that little revenue accrued to the local treasuries since a large proportion of the taxable population was in the plantations.

While Bakweri politicians, such as Manga Williams, intermittently brought up the problem of coastal lands which had been originally alienated to the Germans, it was not until the second world war that the movement became organised and the Bakweri Land Committee was formed. In its petition to the United Nations in August 1946 the committee complained on several counts. They declared that the alienated lands were taken from their people by the Germans without treaty or agreement and wrongfully sold to the plantation companies and missions, in contravention of the principles of customary land law; that the British authorities by recognising the alienation and selling most of the estates back to the Germans perpetuated the wrong acts of the German government; that high profits left the territory from the plantations while the Bakweri people were relegated to poor and difficult land suffering malnutrition and other hardships. They therefore demanded that all the alienated land be returned to them to be developed by the Native Administration on a co-operative basis to the benefit of the people, and that compensation be paid to the Bakweri equal to the proceeds from the plantations during the previous five years and all that was in the plantations. They also demanded that all mission lands except plots on which ecclesiastical and school buildings stood should be returned to the Bakweri people.

Later, when the Cameroons Development Corporation was established, the Bakweri Land Committee sent another petition in which they stated that the CDC which took over the German plantations after the war should be reorganised so that while Europeans might remain at the helm, Africans should at least be appointed in greater number to the Board and others trained in technical and administrative skills in order to assure African control within the next fifteen years.

Indirect rule in the Cameroons

Although the Cameroon was first a mandated and then a Trust Territory under the League of Nations and the United Nations, its general political development was less involved with these two international organisations than with the development of the colonial regimes of Great Britain and France. Each of these European nations came to Africa with a specific viewpoint as to the means and ends of colonialism. These viewpoints, moulded of course by local circumstances, have left an indelible mark on both French- and English-speaking Cameroonians.

Perhaps the most important bastion of British policies in West Africa was the system of indirect rule. In Nigeria Lord Lugard had introduced this system, the essentials being that traditional (or natural) rulers governed their territories under their traditional system with a British official acting as adviser. Practices obnoxious to Europeans, such as slave-raiding and human sacrifices, were abolished and British customs and ideas were either superimposed on, or were blended with, existing traditional ways.

The idea of indirect administration intended that the arrangement of local affairs should be conducted not by foreigners but by persons or classes among the indigenous people who traditionally had authority and command over them. In the early stages of development these persons would undoubtedly be the traditional leaders of indigenous society. What the system ignored, however, is that as this society changed its character, as it did rapidly under the impact of western ideas, power and authority tended to fall into new hands, indirect rule could only succeed where there were traditional rulers to whom the natives owed fealty; it could not persist in conurbations and in places with an African elite who naturally wanted to break with conservatism and who naturally wanted a government of the people for the people by the people and not a government of the people for the people by an individual.

British colonial policy was an empirical one in so far as it never was clear-cut; colonial administrators relied on experience and experiment and not on dogmas or fixed principles. The policy was developed piecemeal at the instance of certain individuals as a panacea to specific problems, and when this worked well, it was applied to similar situations. Indirect rule, of course, was well suited to areas where hierarchical authority structures already existed. It was applied with success in Northern Cameroons, for example, in those areas where traditional Fulani institutions still functioned and also in the central highlands where chiefs had experience of ruling their states with the aid of councillors and police societies. In other areas it was difficult to get the system of indirect rule to work: the 'disturbed' areas of the north inhabited by the non-Muslim pagan peoples are a good example. And in the south there was a confusing number of tribal groups, village groups, clans and chiefdoms, where elders and councils ruled over small communities. It was difficult to assess the extent and nature of a 'chief's' authority in these regions and for this reason the government undertook a systematic series of assessment and intelligence reports to ascertain the authority of traditional rulers, the basis for their power and the role of religious and other social institutions.

Administration

The Northern Cameroons was placed under the Lieutenant-Governor of Northern Nigeria, and Residents administered those parts of the territory which were allotted to the emirates of Bornu and Dikwa and Yola. District heads collected taxes, maintained peace, enforced laws. Indirect rule was applied fairly successfully, although Adamawa proved less receptive to the policy than the Bornu areas, since it had a more heterogeneous population, two-thirds of whom were not Muslims. In the North indirect rule meant strengthening the declining power of the Fulani. Administrative officers were few; economic changes were almost nil. Agriculture and animal husbandry continued in the traditional patterns and education remained in the hands of the *mallams* (Muslim learned men) or of those missionaries permitted to work in the area. Northern Cameroons remained, therefore, isolated, backward, dominated by the Fulani emirates and cut off from the nationalism that was developing in the south, in Cameroons and Nigeria.

South of the Mambila escarpment the country was under the authority of the Lieutenant-Governor of the Southern Provinces (later the Eastern Provinces) of Nigeria, and a Senior Resident ran the affairs of Cameroon Province from Buea. Later, between 1949 and 1954 Bamenda Division was made a province and Kumba, Mamfe and Victoria were administered together as Cameroon Province. The principles of indirect rule formulated to work in hierarchical societies, such as those of the Fulani emirates, were now applied to this area occupied by a variety of tribal groups, only some of which had any degree of centralised authority. These complexities were realised, but funds and personnel were not available to apply direct rule. After a period of intensive reporting on the traditional political systems in these areas, a number of different local authorities were established, some based on traditional chiefs and others on councils, composed of village headmen and councils. The system meant that these local authorities were responsible for various aspects of local government, under the control of district officers; they looked after police, operated courts, collected taxes and dealt with such matters as health, sanitation and roads. The native authorities kept a proportion of the revenue from taxes and court fines.

By 1936 the government had created or recognised a large number of Native Authorities. First of all the Fons of Bali, Kom, Bum and Nsaw in Bamenda and the Fon of Bangwa in Mamfe became Native Authorities, complete with courts and councils. Four chiefs in the southern districts were similarly recognised, including: Chief Manga

The Fon of Bali

Williams, a descendant of King William of Bimbia, and Chief Endeley, the village head of the Bakweri district, who was chief of Buea town. The great majority of the Native Authorities consisted simply of village heads or elders of a village council who were recognised as first among equals (*primus inter pares*). Most Native Authorities were fairly amorphous and necessitated further structural changes along the lines of clan confederacies or federations.

The judicial system involved two sets of courts: the supreme court and magistrates' courts where European-type law was primarily administered; and native courts which were in four grades. 'A' grade courts had full powers in civil cases, while 'B', 'C' and 'D' grade courts could only deal with civil cases in which the claim did not exceed £100, £50 and £25 respectively.

The financial arrangements always depended on the Nigerian central treasury. Perhaps the most common point reiterated by the British and Nigerian Governments when rationalising the integration of the British Cameroons with Nigeria was the assumed fact that the territory was not viable economically. Its budget was subsidised to almost the same amount of revenue received. The Federal Minister of Finance in the House of Representatives in Lagos stated that from 1922 until the outbreak of war in 1939 the former government of Nigeria had spent approximately three quarters of a million pounds more in the Cameroon than it received in revenue. And in 1949, since greater revenue began to come in, any excess of revenue was credited to a special fund to be used for the benefit of the territory.

By the early 1950s Southern Cameroons was administered by a Commissioner and two Residents for the two provinces, Cameroons and Bamenda, and twenty-two district or assistant district officers. The post of Commissioner had been created in 1948 and he was made responsible to the government for dealing locally with all matters arising from the application of the Trusteeship Agreement and for representation of the government at sessions of the Trusteeship Council. In these matters he communicated directly with the Nigerian Government. Up till 1954, as administrative officer in charge of the Cameroons and Bamenda Provinces, he was responsible to the Lieutenant-Governor of the Eastern Region and not to the Governor of Nigeria. He had no administrative responsibility for the Northern Cameroons. When Southern Cameroons became a separate region, he became head of the government of the territory and was directly responsible to the Governor-General in Lagos. However, it should be pointed out that Cameroonian nationalists were not at all content with the appointment of a Commissioner, since they considered him little better than a Resident of a province who could hardly formulate independent policies. The Cameroon Youth League, for example, would have preferred the appointment of an officer who could communicate directly with the United Nations' Trusteeship Council.

CHAPTER 17

British and French rule compared

The French came to Africa on a civilising mission, in so far as the colonies were regarded as France Overseas (*La France d'outre-mer*). The object was to make Cameroun a part of France itself, to persuade the natives to learn the French language, to read French newspapers, attend French schools, adopt French ways of thinking and living and, in short, to turn them into Frenchmen. This was what a French coloniser had in mind when he said: 'France is a nation of 100 million inhabitants'. French settlers mixed freely with colonial peoples, marriages between them were common and in Paris, an Arab from Tunisia or a negro from West Africa felt at home, at least in so far as he had equal rights and privileges with the citizens of France. Those Africans whom the French did succeed in turning into Frenchmen became, on the whole, more loyal to France than British-educated Africans of the same class are to Britain. These assimilated Africans could qualify for full French citizenship; they could also be appointed to posts in the colonial administration equally with citizens of French parentage – they might even rise to be governors of colonies. They could elect deputies to represent them in the French National Assembly and so help to make laws under which they were governed. Nevertheless, the influence of French ideas and civilisation did not succeed in converting many Africans to French ways of life and thought.

The policy of France towards independence for the colonies was thus quite different from that of Britain. The colonies were not prepared for self-government, they were part of France and it was not envisaged that some day they would not be ruled from Paris. It was only afterwards that the French realised their failure to convert Africans into black Frenchmen, since their policy of assimilation and paternalism did not deter the colonies from demanding independence, even if this implied that economically they would have to be tied to the apron strings of the French who would have to subsidise their budgets.

The French system, therefore, did not rely on indirect rule or development from below. The High Commissioner was the representative of the French Government in Paris. The local communes and chief's councils, which were introduced into East Cameroon, never achieved the importance of the West Cameroon counterparts, the House of Chiefs, the native authorities and customary courts. Local government in the east was much more subject to direction and regulation from the centre and indigenous institutions were never developed. The aim was to substitute institutions based on the French model as soon as the people were deemed ready.

An understanding of the differences between French and British attitudes towards the administration of their mandate and trust territories is important in that reunification has brought a confrontation between the results of two very different policies. As we have seen, the British system envisaged an advisory relationship between European political officers and the native authorities, usually chiefs, who were in charge of a local government unit, which corresponded to a traditional political unit: a Bamenda state, a group of Mamfe villages. In the French system the chief or the local council was always entirely subordinate to the European political agent. The chief in East Cameroon was an agent of the colonial government and he did not necessarily administer an area which corresponded to a traditional chiefdom or village area. The French divided up the country into equal, logical administrative areas which often cut across traditional political boundaries; these were *départements* (or regions), *arrondissements* (or districts) and communes. Neither practically nor in theory did the French envisage the policy of using African institutions nor encouraging African culture. Even the chiefs as agents of the central government were frequently men who would never have traditionally been appointed to chieftainship. And as intermediaries of the French they were obliged to be loyal to the colonial government and hence were often obliged to ignore advice from traditional councils.

It is perhaps in the difference in attitudes to traditional chiefs that French and British theories of colonialisation differ the most. In West Cameroon and Nigeria chiefs were men of importance who were highly respected by European and African alike, whereas their counterparts in the French territory were shorn of economic privilege and political power. A Fon, under the British, for example, was a man of importance, with a staff and salary; politically and administratively he was the king-pin of his region. He was the proud head of a state,

Charles Atangana

allowed to retain economic prerogative and given a part to play in the administration of the country. Over the border in East Cameroon, the counterparts of the Fons were more often than not appointees of the French, or if not, were cut off from their old tributary monies, and their servants and their essential ceremonies and rites were curtailed. Again, however, it is difficult to say which side will be proved right in the long run: the British who propped up the declining feudal institutions of the nineteenth century in the interest of a smooth changeover from the old world to the new; or the French who preferred a sudden break in the interests of efficiency.

In French Cameroon, therefore, chiefs were usually created by the French administration for purely administrative purposes. Sometimes a local village chief in a region was given extended powers over a much wider region. Or the French merely appointed a man they thought they could trust. The most notable example of such an artificial chief was Charles Atangana, an interpreter and primary school teacher, who had been a lieutenant in the German army. The Germans had made him chief of the Ewondo (Yaounde) people. After the war, and a period of internment, he was reinstated by the French, who even extended his authority to cover other tribes. He became rich and powerful and a highly respected chief and public servant; when he died in 1943 a statue was erected to his honour in Yaounde.

In contrast we have the story of the well-known Sultan Njoya of Bamum, who after a long and successful reign was deposed and exiled by the French in 1931. He had maintained his throne through a long period of German, British and French colonial rule, but his originality along with his traditional autocracy brought him into conflict with the French administration, and their ideas of the role to be played by African chiefs. The French tried to counter his influence by designating chiefs to rule over provinces within Bamum and forcing them to become entirely dependent on the colonial government instead of the Bamum king. Njoya sought to make the people rebel against this situation, but the French reacted by cutting him off from his traditional tribute monies. After a six-year fight the Sultan was exiled to Yaounde, where he lived on a French pension until he died.

Assimilation and the law

Although the aim of French colonial policy was the assimilation of Africans to French language and culture – that is, their conversion into black Frenchmen (*évolués*) – in fact assimilation was never widely applied, nor was it a practical possibility. Assimilation existed only in so far as it created an elite of *évolués* who were set off from the vast masses of the population (the *indigènes*). The latter did not have the benefit of the rights of the French legal system and were subject to a separate legal regime known as the *indigénat*.

The *indigénat* was a legal system whereby, in tune with the French policy of assimilating educated elements, a distinction was made between ordinary subjects who were subject to native custom and assimilated citizens who were given civil and political rights, identical to persons of French origin. The differentiation was made according to the standards of a person's achievement of French culture. Through the *indigénat* a system of summary punishment was applied only to non-assimilated Cameroonians. There was an extraordinary variety of acts and misdemeanours which could be thus punished without trial: from 'acts of disorder' and 'gambling' to 'vagabondage' and a 'refusal to pay taxes'. It was a very unjust system and one which was finally condemned by the French administrators who attended the Brazzaville conference in 1944. It was also entirely arbitrary, any administrator having the right to inflict punishment for a vaguely defined list of punishments. On the whole the *indigénat* was used to punish natives who failed to work their farms or pay their taxes. The system engendered such antagonism that it was eventually abolished in 1946.

Closely associated with the *indigénat* in many ways was the French system of forced labour known as *prestation*. The French used forced labour in the Cameroon during the early years of the administration when major railway and road projects were undertaken. The antagonism aroused by this among many Cameroonian tribes, particularly in the south, lasted for many years. *Prestation* itself was a kind of compulsory labour obligation whereby all males were obliged to furnish the government with ten days' free labour a year; if they remained on the job after ten days, they were paid a minimal wage set at so much per kilometre of road or track finished. It is difficult not to see this as a continuation of the German labour tax. Initially recruitment was done through local chiefs, but when the chiefs began to recruit free labour for their own private purposes the administration handed over the task to government administrators.

In general the French system worked efficiently in East Cameroon, despite the abuses mentioned. Progress was made in various non-political fields, particularly in education and health. Educational standards were higher in Cameroon than in any other French West African territory and, under the leadership of Dr. Eugene Jamot, sleeping-sickness was entirely eradicated. Economic developments were relatively modest up till the second world war, when France undertook measures to promote economic and social advancement on a much larger scale, financing its plans in large part by grants and loans from the French treasury.

Compared with British Cameroons, the French territory seemed a paradise of progress to young English-speaking Cameroonians. They saw the building of ports and railways, fine hard-surfaced roads, large European-staffed shops, hotels, water supplies and electricity. They saw that French settlers ran plantations and had farms, cooked in restaurants, butchered and carried on petty trading. Mineral resources were being exploited by French companies. The country became rapidly urbanised in towns like Edea, Yaounde, Ebolowa, Nkongsamba, Dschang and Foumban. Douala tripled in population in twelve years.

As a result of this progress large numbers of Cameroonians left the rural areas and moved to the towns. Some 100,000 Bamileke emigrated from their home regions in the twenty-five years after 1931, for example, and in Douala their number rose from 8,000 in 1947 to almost 30,000 in 1956, even outnumbering the Douala people. The Bamileke also had the greatest number of employees in the administration, banking, commerce, transport and industries; they also, as a result, constituted a large proportion of the unemployed, so that many Cameroonians began to press for political reform and eventual independence from French rule.

Southern Cameroons seemed to be a rather primitive backwater, with poor communications, no railways or main roads. In the provision of other amenities such as hospitals, schools, hotels, etc., the British Cameroons certainly lagged behind the French. There were perhaps some advantages, however. The British system of indirect rule was a humane one, and there was certainly no system remotely approaching the French *indigénat* which virtually deprived French Cameroonians of their liberty of criticism, association and movement. The British never empowered their agents or deputies to inflict disciplinary penalties for a wide range of offences, without trial. Nor did the British ever try to reconstitute the German system of forced labour in their public works, except in so far as prisoners were used on local construction programmes. Politically the territory was more advanced than French Cameroon as the British did encourage the participation of Africans in local government, in councils and prepared the inhabitants for eventual self-government.

The English-speaking Cameroonian, certainly less sophisticated than his French-speaking compatriot, became imbued with a particularly British way of life: a way of life which most educated Cameroonians, even those most appreciative of progress in East Cameroon and bitterly opposed to British administration, have continued to appreciate. While unfavourable comparisons are easily made with the progress achieved in East Cameroon by the French, it should be remembered that this progress in many ways depended on allowing non-Cameroonians to settle, buy lands and exploit the country's resources in their own interests. In British Cameroons, the Europeans were civil servants, priests and traders, all of whom were only temporary residents in the country. While this did not lead to industrialisation and urbanisation, it did mean that there was no racial antipathy and Cameroonians in the West moved painlessly into the modern world. This is one of the reasons for the calm situation in the British Cameroons before and after reunification, where there was no hint of the violent and bitter strife which rent the Cameroon Republic in the east.

CHAPTER 18

Early political developments

The Clifford Constitution

In 1922, the same year that Britain received a mandate from the League of Nations to administer the British Cameroons as an integral part of Nigeria, the first constitutional changes in Nigeria occurred with the implementation of the Clifford Constitution. This set up a Legislative Council comprising the Governor, as President, a maximum of thirty official members, three elected, non-official members, representing the municipal area of Lagos and one representing the municipal area of Calabar. There were also fifteen nominated unofficial members.

At the time, the Governor, Clifford, even claimed that this constitution with its elective principle was only the first step towards complete self-government and later events were to lead to the extension of the elective principle to more backward parts of the Nigerian protectorate and Cameroons.

With the prospect of acquiring some seats on the Legislative Council, parties were formed in Lagos and newspapers were produced to champion their respective causes. In the 1923 election Herbert Macaulay's party, the National Democratic Party, won the three seats, taking them again in 1929 and 1933. However, there was little scope for political activity in towns which had no representation in the Council; politics until the late '30s were, therefore, mainly confined to Lagos and its problems. At various constitutional conferences the Southern Cameroons were able to achieve some constitutional advancement as a province of Nigeria. However, throughout this time the territory as a unit remained in a disadvantageous position; the larger provinces had much better representation and Cameroons always remained on the outskirts of developments in Nigeria as a whole.

The second world war and the United Nations

The second world war is an important dividing mark in the history of Cameroon politics. In the post-war period a new political order developed; political leaders in the Cameroons and Nigeria began to press their claims for responsible government and, later, for Southern Cameroons to be recognised as a country in its own right. One aspect of the second world war and the participation of many Cameroonians as soldiers was the sudden appreciation by Africans that Europeans were not all stand-offish governors, army officers, administrative officers, but that there were common men with white skins – farmers, miners, servants. Cameroonians served alongside white soldiers and these soldiers arrived in the Cameroons with no more privileges than the local soldiery.

At the same time general criticisms of colonialism began to be made throughout the world, particularly in America, and the third clause of the Atlantic Charter which assured the 'right of all peoples to choose the form of government under which they live . . .' spurred Cameroonian nationalists to hope for self-government in the future. In England, too, Labour politicians were pressing for further political progress in the colonies.

The political consciousness which began to develop among Cameroonians for the first time was to some extent supported by expatriate administrators. The poor communications, particularly the separation of the Bamenda Plateau from the coast, were considered to be scandalous. In the east things also began to stir and settlers from Cameroon in the west formed the French Cameroons Welfare Union. After the war there also came a certain economic development. Already in 1943 a development plan had been proposed by the provincial Resident and in 1949 the ex-German plantations were handed over to the Nigerian Government for the benefit of the Trust Territory.

The trusteeship system of the United Nations introduced new elements into the system of international supervision set up by the League. Thus the UN charter said that trusteeship was intended to promote the political, economic social and educational advancement of the inhabitants of the territory and their development towards self-government or independence. The system effectively brought pressure to bear on the administering authorities, involving annual reports and on-the-spot investigations. Between 1949 and 1958, four missions were sent to the Cameroons to investigate the way the trustee was performing its role. The missions received detailed reports and petitions from individuals and political parties seeking relief from grievances and commenting on the political situation. The purpose of the reports was to ensure that the provisions of the Trusteeship Agreement were adhered to, and to assess the pace of development socially, economically, politically and otherwise of the country on the road to self-determination. A special representative of the administering authority answered oral questions concerning the reports on the administration of the territory put by members of the council.

Visits were made by Visiting Missions of the UNO to the Cameroons in 1949, 1952, 1955 and 1958. These visits were valuable in that they spotlighted many things which the administering authority was quite oblivious of, and they gave local inhabitants the opportunity to present petitions direct to members of UNO. For example, petitions were forwarded about the Bakweri land problem; and the Kamerun United National Congress petitioned, among other things, that barriers to free movement from British to French Cameroons be removed, that a separate House of Assembly for the British Cameroons should be created and that there should be compulsory instruction in English and French in both Cameroons.

The United Nations afforded the inhabitants of the territories the opportunity to make statements to the committee and, in this way, politicians were able to impress their viewpoint on the world body. Mr Um Nyobe and Mr Okala, representing the Union des Populations du Cameroun and the Partie Socialiste Camerounaise respectively, spoke on 17 December 1952, the former in favour of unification, the latter against it. The plebiscites, which were held in Northern and Southern Cameroons were also organised and supervised by the United Nations. In general, Cameroonians were placed in a more advantageous position than other colonial territories in that they had the opportunity to present their cases, either domestic or national, to arbitration at the United Nations and the system of annual reports made it possible to assess what the administering authority had achieved in the territory.

Cameroonian politicians

At about the time of the second world war, a number of young Cameroonian students and intellectuals began to organise various kinds of common interest or welfare associations among themselves, which encouraged the discussion of political matters. The most important of these associations were organised outside Cameroon itself, in Nigeria mainly, where their leaders were studying or working. The best known of these groups was the Cameroons Youth League (CYL), founded in 1939 by Peter M. Kale and Emmanuel Endeley, the two most important political figures in the early days of Cameroonian political developments.

Kale had worked as a teacher in Buea and Mamfe from 1929 to 1935 before going to Nigeria and teaching in the Salvation Army School in Lagos. As founder and president of the CYL he represented Cameroon interests in the National Council of Nigeria and the Cameroons (NCNC), which he helped to form in 1944. The stated aims of the CYL were to arouse a national consciousness among Cameroonians and to achieve a recognised status for the territory. Shortly after World War II he wrote a booklet which had an important influence on his fellow intellectuals and aimed at helping Cameroonians understand their country's background and the significance of their future. Foncha, who was also a founder-member of the CYL, has said that it was this book which 'kindled in him the spirit of the Cameroons nation'. Kale remained a highly respected and popular leader throughout the vicissitudes of post-war politics. At the plebiscite in 1961 he appeared in Cameroon politics as a proponent of separate independence for British Cameroons, but he received no support. After reunification his work on behalf of Cameroons emancipation was recognised when he became Speaker of the West Cameroon Assembly.

Endeley was born in 1916, the son of the chief of Buea Town, who received his primary education in Cameroon and then went to Yaba Higher College near Lagos. He qualified as a doctor but continued to play an important role in Cameroons politics, playing an important part in the founding of the NCNC with P.M. Kale. After leaving the medical profession he returned to Buea and became involved in political and trade union activities. In September 1947 he was general secretary of the Cameroon Development Corporation Workers' Union and later became the moving spirit of the Bakweri Land Claims Committee.

The arrival on the scene of men like Kale and Endeley was a sign of the changes taking place in Cameroonian and Nigerian politics. In Nigeria a new generation of politicians began to replace the closed group of educated Africans who came from the upper-class Creole or Yoruba families which had long been in contact with Europeans. Most of the new men were, like Kale and Endeley, students or graduates, and student organisations were the main elements involved in this growing spirit of nationalism.

Politically, however, most Nigerian and Cameroonian people were powerless. It was only in 1943, for example, that Nigerians were appointed to the executive council, and then they were usually 'safe government men'. The failure of the British to allow the educated elite to participate in the country's affairs resulted in increasingly virulent attacks by nationalists on the British administration.

In the mid-forties Cameroonian politics became bound up with a new Nigerian party: the National Council of Nigeria and the Cameroons, which was founded in 1944 by Kale, Endeley, Nnamdi Azikiwe and older political leaders such as Herbert Macaulay. The NCNC was not really a party, but a confederation of trade unions, smaller parties, tribal unions and groups such as the Cameroons Youth League. In January 1945 it held its first constitutional convention in which it proclaimed its intention to 'achieve internal self-government for Nigeria whereby the people of Nigeria and the Cameroons under British Mandate shall exercise executive legislative and judicial powers'. (Constitution of the NCNC Lagos, p. 1).

The Richards Constitution

The new political awareness played a part in post-war constitutional advances made when Sir Arthur Richards, Governor of Nigeria, introduced his new constitution, which came into effect on January 1 1947. The new legislative council was enlarged to forty-four members with a majority of unofficials, twenty-eight as against sixteen official. Of these twenty-eight, however, only four were elected, the rest being nominated or indirectly elected. The most important feature as far as Nigeria was concerned was the inclusion of the North in the Central Legislature, a move aimed at furthering the unity of the country. At the same time regional councils were created for the north, east and west. The Regional Houses of Assembly performed advisory functions and they were intended to serve as a link between the Native Authorities and the Legislative Council. They were to consider and advise by resolution on any matters referred to them by the Governor or introduced by a member in accordance with the provisions of the Order-in-Council creating the Houses.

The Cameroons, of course, had no regional government. It was represented in the Eastern House of Assembly by Chief Manga Williams and Galega, the Fon of Bali. Apart from them it comprised the Chief Commissioner of Eastern Nigeria as President, thirteen other official members, fifteen to eighteen unofficial members from the provinces of which ten to thirteen were selected by Native Authorities and five nominated by the Governor from interests and communities, who were nevertheless inadequately represented. The nominated members were official nominees and held their office at the pleasure of the Governor.

In order that the Legislative Council should be more representative of the whole country and its interests, the constitution provided for the regions to be represented by four chiefs, nominated by the Northern House of Chiefs; five members nominated by the Northern House of Assembly; four members nominated by the Western House of Assembly; five by the Eastern House; two chiefs nominated from those already members of the Western House; and one from the colony area. Despite its defects, the constitution served as a catalyst in Nigerian politics by creating unity out of diversity. For the first time Nigerian legislators from all over the country met and became acquainted, learnt each other's hopes and plans. Moreover one of the most significant aspects of the Richards Constitution and its regional councils was the incorporation of the Native Administration system ('Indirect Rule'), the main feature of British rule in Africa, into the constitutional structure of the country. The scope of the activities of natural rulers was no longer confined to villages and tribes, but was widened so that they could play a part in national affairs.

This Richards Constitution was, of course, an advance on anything achieved beforehand in Nigeria, but it was criticised by all Nigerians involved. Chief Awolowo criticised the imbalance in the ratio of representatives to populations: one to nearly 800,000 people in the north and one to almost 400,000 in the east. He also condemned the system of nominating, instead of electing, members and felt that in view of the diverse culture in Nigeria, it was anachronistic to have a unitary constitution in the country. The NCNC bitterly complained that the Governor had not consulted public opinion, and attacked as false the so-called majorities of unofficial members in central and regional assemblies, since many of the so-called 'unofficials' were nominated or were quasi-officials like chiefs and native authority members. They also pointed out that the Executive Council remained wholly European.

Post-war politics

The Richards Constitution and the famous 'four obnoxious ordinances' (dealing with land and mining rights and appointments of chiefs) were the springboard for the beginning of a spirited political agitation in Nigeria and Cameroons in the post-war period. The NCNC in particular took up the issues involved in the Richards Constitution and began to instil into the people a sense of political awareness. Many Cameroonians maintained that the constitution represented a backward step in their own country in so far as they now lost representation at the centre. Previously they had had a single representative, Chief Manga Williams of Victoria, in the Legislative Council. During this period attempts had been made to suggest that other incumbents be nominated for Chief Williams' seat, but these had been ignored by the British. Now with the Richards Constitution, while providing for the election of up to thirteen members of the Eastern Regional House of Assembly by native authorities (two from the Southern Cameroons), all representation of the Southern Cameroons at the centre was abolished.

The campaign against the Richards Constitution was well organised, resulting in tours of Nigeria and the Cameroons and eventually the journey of a delegation to England. The tour had important effects, particularly in Cameroons, where it rallied the people to a common political cause and helped to emphasise the identity of the Cameroons as a separate entity. The leading Cameroonian member of the delegation was P.M. Kale, the founder of the Cameroons Youth League, who, along with Dr Azikiwe, presented a Memorandum to the Labour Colonial Secretary, Sir Arthur Creech Jones. Kale was determined to pinpoint the problems facing the Cameroons, such as their inadequate representation in the Nigerian Legislative Assemblies, the land problem and the lack of educational and other facilities.

The NCNC delegation arrived in London in August 1947 and presented their memorandum to the Colonial Secretary. It demanded immediate steps to be taken towards self-government for Nigerian and Cameroonian peoples. In particular the NCNC delegation objected to the constitution because the eighteen chiefs and native authority members who were African-nominated unofficial members could be removed at the sole pleasure of the Governor, in whose appointment and tenure of office the taxpayers of Nigeria had no voice; and it was therefore impossible for the official nominees to exercise freedom of speech in the interest of taxpayers, especially in matters in which the government was interested. Furthermore, the seven remaining unofficial members, three of them non-Africans, also held office and could be removed at the pleasure of the Governor.

The NCNC delegation made some new and positive proposals in their memorandum. They maintained that all land in Nigeria and the Cameroons, whether occupied or not, should be declared native land and that all rights of ownership over native land should be vested in the indigenous inhabitants as being inalienable and untransferable. They argued that the government could acquire land and use it for the settlement of 'people of African descent' and that this could be construed to imply that immigrant races could settle in

Nigeria with the attendant humiliating racial situations of the kind found in East Africa, Southern Rhodesia and South Africa.

The NCNC also declared itself against the legal principle which gave the Governor power to be 'sole judge of what was native law and custom, and in the case of dispute the Governor had power to depose chiefs, which was an interference with traditional laws and customs of the people'. Other examples of the denial of basic human rights included the Governor's power to grant or withhold a licence for a press publication; the punishment by fine or imprisonment of workers who went on strike while doing essential work without giving sufficient notice of their intention to strike; the absolute power of the police to prevent any person leaving or entering Nigeria if he were suspected of being undesirable; the Governor's power to prohibit worship if he considered it a breach of the peace; or to close any school if the Director of Education considered the proprietor or director undesirable.

Various cases of maladministration were enumerated. Nigerians in the Nigeria Regiment could not become commissioned officers no matter how well educated or fitted they were for the job. Europeans were employed at comparatively high salaries to fill vacancies in the civil service to the exclusion of Nigerian unemployed youths and ex-servicemen. Chiefs had been subjected to deportation, deposition and arrest when suspected of being disrespectful, or engaged in activities considered subversive.

The Kale Memorandum

At the same time the Kale Memorandum brought up many points which rankled with Southern Cameroonians. Kale stressed the fact that the division of German Kamerun between France and Britain had divided families and made them strangers to each other despite linguistic and tribal affinity. He also claimed that Northern and Southern Cameroons were big enough to be administered as a single entity. Kale claimed that the alienation of land in Victoria and Kumba divisions by the Germans had reduced the people to serfdom; in order to improve their situation all land in the territory should be known as native land and all land taken from the Bakweri should be returned to them and be looked after by the Native Administration on a co-operative basis, with any profits to be used for the benefit of the people. Proceeds which had accrued from the plantations for five years should be paid to the people as compensation for the exploitation of the land. All mission land should also be returned to the Bakweri, the memorandum stated, except where churches and schools had been built. Kale pointed out that no Bakweri person was a member of the Board of the Cameroons Development Corporation. The memorandum claimed that of all those children who left primary school in Cameroons only about 2% had the advantage of secondary schooling, and this had to be achieved by going to Nigeria. Two secondary schools, one for boys and one for girls, were proposed for the territory with twenty annual scholarships.

Unfortunately the Colonial Secretary's reaction to the delegation's demands was merely to urge them to return home and give the Richards Constitution a trial. At the same time the delegates began to quarrel among themselves and returned home to Nigeria to face a barrage of criticism from NCNC members for squandering the £13,000 which had been collected from the people before the delegation's visit to Great Britain.

CHAPTER 19

Cameroonian nationalism in the Southern Cameroons

The Macpherson Constitution

The Richards Constitution was originally to have remained in force for nine years but already in 1948 the new Labour-appointed Governor, Sir John Macpherson, announced that progress had been so good that the country was ripe for a change. This time he did not make the same mistake as his predecessor of not consulting public opinion; in fact discussions and negotiation went on for two years and the people were consulted at every level. In Nigeria and in the Cameroons, village councils sent delegates to divisional councils, then to provincial and regional councils and finally to a general conference at Ibadan. At a provincial conference for the Cameroons Province for example, which assembled at Mamfe at the end of June 1948, the views of villages and divisional meetings and representative organisations were considered. It included members of the provincial meeting, representatives of tribal unions and youth organisations.

Among the resolutions there was a demand for complete regional status for the Trust Territory. During the three years of debate about the new constitution, the question of regional status for the Southern Cameroons was constantly brought up. Early in 1949, the Cameroons Provincial Council, comprising twenty-seven chiefs, six administrative officers and thirty-seven observers, met in Victoria under the chairmanship of Chief Manga Williams and adopted a resolution for a separate regional government for the territory. In March 1949 a combined body of Cameroons organisations in Lagos, consisting of the Mamfe Improvement Union, the Cameroons Youth League, the Bamenda Improvement Association and the Bakweri Union, petitioned the Governor for a separate Cameroons region with a separate House of Assembly under a Chief Commissioner to be directly responsible to the Trusteeship Council.

At the same time the first arguments began to be heard in favour of reunification with the French Trust Territory of Cameroun. In

May 1949 Dr Endeley sponsored a conference of political parties from both British and French Cameroons at Chief Mukete's house in Kumba, where together with UPC leaders they agreed to work steadfastly to achieve a unified Cameroon. The plan that seemed to have emerged at this meeting was that both sectors should first of all achieve independence, after which unification would follow as a matter of course. Many of the delegates from the Southern Cameroons argued that since socially, economically and politically British Cameroons stood far behind, any premature unification would have the effect of making Southern Cameroons a protectorate of French Cameroon.

Meanwhile, in the north the demands for the creation of a separate Cameroons region had not found any response. The Northern Provincial Constitutional meeting, comprising representatives from the Northern Cameroons, resolved that the Trust Territory of the Cameroons in the Northern Region should continue to be administered as part of the Northern Region and that trusteeship should be ended. At this Northern Regional Conference there were only two representatives from the Northern Cameroons: the emir of Dikwa and his chief scribe who declared themselves in favour of trusteeship being continued. They were overruled by the delegates from outside the Cameroons who formed the majority. As far as the Northern Cameroons was concerned this was the last opportunity for the views of the people to be heard, since they were not represented at later draftings and general conferences.

The proposal that the Southern Cameroons should separate from the Eastern Region was examined at the Eastern Regional Conference held at Enugu in July 1949. After a sympathetic hearing it was decided that the position of the Cameroons as a separate region would be unsound and politically difficult to organise in view of the position of that part of the Trust Territory which was administered as part of the Northern Region. The conference did suggest, however, that the demands of the Cameroons and Bamenda Provinces might satisfactorily be met by representation of the Trust Territory in both the regional House of Assembly and Executive Council and in the new central executive and legislature.

In January 1950 the General Conference met at Ibadan. The Southern Cameroons were represented by two officials of the Cameroons National Federation, one of whom was Dr Endeley. The Ibadan conference accepted the views of both the Eastern and Northern Regional Conferences on the country's status. The representatives from the Cameroons later complained that in view of their minority position at the conference, dominated by Nigerian delegates, they could not press effectively for a separate regional organisation for the Trust Territory. After the decisions of the conference had been debated in the Regional Houses, the final recommendations were approved by the Secretary of State for the Colonies. The proposals under the Macpherson Constitution for the represen- tation of the Cameroons and Bamenda Provinces were as follows: in the Eastern House of Assembly they were to have thirteen members in a House of approximately eighty members and one senior regional official with no vote. The House of Representatives was to have two members to be selected from the Cameroons which was administered as part of the Eastern Region. In the Council of Ministers, of the four Ministers from the Eastern Region there was to be one for the Cam- eroons.

The constitution came into effect in 1952 and the first elections were contested on party lines in the Regions, resulting in the success of the Action Group in the Western Region, the NCNC in the Eastern Region and the NPC in the north. In the Cameroons there were two political parties, the Cameroon National Federation and the Kam- erun United National Congress. The need to discuss proposals for the MacPherson Constitution and also send petitions to the United Nations Missions, which arrived in the country to investigate the Trust Territories' affairs, had led to the formation of the Cameroons National Federation in May 1949. This grouped some twenty ethnic 'Improvement Unions' along with the CDC union and other trade unions as well as land committees. It also included representatives of French-speaking Cameroonians resident in the British Trust area. The CNF not only aimed at a separate region for Southern Camer- oons but also claimed that it would mean the beginning of a struggle for unification with their 'brothers under the French – the dream of every living Cameroonian'.

The second party, the KUNC, was founded in August 1951. This party also had connections with the neighbouring Trust Territory, primarily with the UPC (see p. 147). Its aims were also to obtain regional status for the British Cameroons inside Nigeria, with the ultimate objective of reunification with the Cameroon under French administration. The rise of the KUNC, led by R.J.K. Dibonge and N.N. Mbile, meant the decline in the influence of the Cameroons National Federation. Dibonge was one of the earliest and foremost of Cameroonian nationalists. He had been educated in Germany and occupied important posts under the French, then under the British in Buea. In 1944 he had been chief clerk in Enugu but returned to

Dr Endeley

Douala in 1947 and then Victoria in 1949. In that year he founded the French Cameroons Welfare Union (FCWU). In founding a party in opposition to Endeley's CNF he was supported by N.N. Mbile who was Endeley's successor as General Secretary of the CDC Workers' Union – and by Foncha. The differences between the two parties were not very noticeable at the time, nevertheless it was the first of several splits which brought politicians like Endeley and Foncha on to opposing sides in Southern Cameroons' politics.

The 1950 elections were the first the territory had known and surprisingly little interest was shown in them. Only 25 to 30% cast their votes and the figures were sometimes as low as 10%. In Mamfe Division, for example, out of fifty primary units, only nine were

N.N. Mbile

contested and in the Kumba Division the number was as low as two and in Victoria three. In Victoria the elections were remarkable for the defeat of Chief Manga Williams. In the Central Council of Ministers, Dr Endeley became Minister Without Portfolio. In the Eastern Executive Council S.T. Muna became Minister of Works. Of the thirteen Cameroon members elected to the Eastern House of Assembly, six (the Rev. J. Kangsen, J. Ndze, S.T. Muna, S.A. George, Dr Endeley and N.N. Mbile) were elected to the Central House of Representatives.

Even though, as we have seen, there were two political parties, the CNF and the KUNC, in Southern Cameroons at this time, most of those who won the election did so on their individual merits. When the Cameroon representatives entered the Eastern House of Assembly each declared for the NCNC, the party in power in the Eastern Region, although they had, of course, received no mandate to do so from their constitutents. This had important consequences since as a result of their commitment they became involved, willy-nilly, in the maelstrom of Nigerian politics and the ensuing crisis in the House of Assembly. Nevertheless the association seemed increasingly in the nature of a marriage of convenience, and politicians such as Foncha, S.A. George and S.T. Muna who sat in the Nigerian legislatures under the NCNC banner, began to express their dislike of the connection.

In the short period between the 1950 elections and the 1953 crisis, Cameroon representatives in both the eastern and central legislatures began to press for a recognition of the Cameroons as a separate entity, an entity which had been cruelly forgotten by the British and the central government in the preceding years. A speech by S.A. George in the House of Representatives at Lagos shows the attitudes of these representatives and their attempts to project the image of the Territory and its needs, particularly within Nigeria. George spoke about the need of development in Cameroons, and the period of neglect which the Territory had experienced up till the Trust period.

The Territory was looked after and essential administrative services were maintained on a skeleton basis for twenty-eight years. For this period also, the Cameroons was subjected to vigorous, merciless exploitation while its inhabitants lived merely as plantation slaves under German farmers. Britain allowed the German Government and her subjects to use the Territory as a supply house for all the rubber, banana, cocoa and other products which made Germany confident in her second onslaught on civilisation. Provision of social services were unknown and unheard of in the Cameroons. There was no link with Nigeria for fear that Germany might ultimately take back full political control of the Territory.

The Territory plodded on and on. Her inhabitants were semi-educated, attending such schools as poor funds of the native authorities could provide and receiving higher elementary education from the divisional government school that the Education Department maintained in the Territory. Her petty traders were half-naked, daring trekkers from the hills of Bamenda who spent their lives on jungle tracks, crossing dangerous streams to the port of Calabar to buy their merchandise for exchange among their people.

It was the custom then for civil servants in Nigeria to resign their appointments when they were requested to proceed on transfer to the Cameroons. It was known to be a country isolated from Nigeria to arrive at which no less than two weeks' journey would be made on foot through dangerous country.

As recently as 1946 I personally made a journey from Kumba to Mamfe on foot, a distance of 120 miles, carrying my load on my own head. Today vast numbers in the Territory still do the same thing. A larger proportion of the northern section is still regarded as an unsettled area today because the new way of life that banishes crudity and barbarism has not up till now been introduced there.

The 1953 political crisis in Nigeria

The Macpherson Constitution, liberal compared with its predecessors, was destined to last only a short time, mainly due to a new political situation and also because the new constitution was a compromise. The particular defect of the constitution was the lack of ministerial responsibility, ministers acting as spokesmen for their department but having no responsibility for policy formation.

The Eastern Regional Crisis of 1953 which led to the breakdown of the Macpherson Constitution, concerned a challenge to Azikiwe's leadership of the party. It caused a rift in the NCNC, the resignation of the government, legislative paralysis and eventually the dissolution of the House of Assembly. In the party there had been sharp disagreement between members holding ministerial office in the Eastern and Central Houses among those who wanted to give the constitution a fair trial and those who wanted to withdraw their support. In December 1952 the three NCNC central ministers were expelled from the party although Dr Endeley was unaffected by these dismissals, because he was a minister not on the NCNC ticket but as a representative of the Cameroons.

In May 1953 a motion in the Eastern House of Assembly, that Muna be reinstated in the Eastern Cabinet was defeated by 45 votes to 32 and this caused a great deal of frustration among Southern Cameroonian members of the House who had earlier wanted to declare their 'benevolent neutrality' in Nigerian politics. They walked out of the Eastern House of Assembly and decided that they would boycott elections to the Eastern House of Assembly since they had broken their connection with the Eastern region because they believed that as a minority group in the Eastern Regional Legislature they were unable to make the wishes of Cameroon people respected. They considered it necessary to press for a separate region and called on all Cameroonians to boycott any future elections to the Eastern House of Assembly until they were granted their own House of Assembly. All native authorities, tribal organisations, chiefs and people of every village and town were asked to send two representatives each to a conference to be held in May 1953.

The significance of this crisis for the Cameroons is that it gave Cameroonian politicians the chance to break away from the NCNC. When the conference met in Mamfe the Kamerun United National Congress and the Cameroons National Federation were called upon to merge. The statement signifying this merger was signed by Mr Dibonge for the KUNC and Dr Endeley for the CNF. Endeley, Muna and Foncha became the backbone of the new party, known as the Kamerun National Congress (KNC). Mbile, who was Secretary-General of the KUNC, was relieved of his post and dismissed from the party. With Kale he formed the Kamerun People's Party (KPP), which urged the retention of the NCNC links under Azikiwe and continued in association with the Eastern Region.

This was almost the end of Cameroonian participation in the affairs of the Nigerian NCNC Party. The NCNC had developed into a predominantly Ibo organisation; Azikiwe was himself an Ibo and became more and more a leader of the Ibos, their saviour who would put an end to their lower status in Nigeria, particularly in the sphere of higher education. For many Cameroonians, therefore, the NCNC was seen to be too much of an Ibo party, and with the increasing prejudice against Ibo immigration workers, traders and civil servants, Cameroon politicians began to create independent political parties to work for the interests of the Cameroons.

The Lyttelton Constitution

After the crisis in the Eastern Region House of Assembly which led to the collapse of the Macpherson Constitution and produced serious divisions among the Southern Cameroons' representatives, there came a period in which serious pressure began to build up in the territory for separate institutions of its own. The increasing agitation within the Cameroons for separate political institutions was reflected in the constitutional conferences held in London in August 1953 and later in Lagos in January 1954. At the London conference both the Southern and Northern Cameroons were given the opportunity of stating their points of view. Dr Endeley, this time supported by Mr Mbile, had hoped that the Southern and Northern Cameroons could be brought together to form a separate region, but the Northern Cameroons delegation made it clear that they wished to continue their present association with the Northern Region. Nevertheless Dr Endeley received provisional acceptance of his demands for a separate region for the Southern Cameroons with their own small-scale legislature and executive and with suitable representation in the Central Nigerian Legislature and Council of Ministers. However, no decision was to be made until the outcome of the General Election which Dr Endeley would fight on this issue.

In the Southern Cameroons both the KNC and the KPP campaigned vigorously. The KNC referred to Ibo domination and to the advantages to be gained from the two provinces having their own territorial assembly. The KPP, on the other hand, told the people that the Southern Cameroons would not be financially viable as a separate unit and urged that the best course of action would be for the territory to be administered as part of the Eastern Region. In the election campaigns Dr Azikiwe, along with top members of the NCNC, campaigned for Mbile and the other KPP candidates. In several places Azikiwe was heckled by his audience because they said he was supporting those who 'wanted to sell Cameroons to the Ibos'. In the event, the KNC won twelve of the thirteen seats in the East Regional Legislatures and, accordingly, it was announced at the Lagos constitutional conference that Southern Cameroons would be separated from the Eastern Region, remaining part of Nigeria as a quasi-federal territory.

The phrase 'quasi-federal territory' meant that both the Federal Legislature and the Federal Executive would retain jurisdiction in the territory with respect to matters within their competence, that laws would still require the assent of the Governor-General, but that there would be a House of Assembly consisting of the Commissioner of the Cameroons, as President, and three *ex-officio* members; two representatives of special interests (who would be nominated); six representatives of the native authorities; and thirteen elected members. The legislature was given power to raise taxes and legislate on subjects on the 'concurrent list' (shared with the federal authorities) and residual matters in terms of the Nigerian constitution. The Executive Council was to consist of four official and four unofficial members, including the Commissioner. It was to elect six members to the Nigerian Federal Legislature. The Federal Legislature and Federal Executive were to have jurisdiction in the territory with respect to Federal matters.

The first meeting of the Southern Cameroons House of Assembly was held on 26 October 1954, a date later commemorated as Southern Cameroons National Day. The Executive Council, in addition to the Commissioner, the Deputy Commissioner, the Legal Secretary and the Financial and Developmental Secretary, included Dr Endeley as Leader of Government Business, S.A. George, the Rev. J. Kangsen and S.T. Muna. It should be pointed out that although the Southern Cameroons had achieved separation from Eastern Nigeria, the territory's government did not have all the accoutrements of regionalism. There was no public service commission, and Cameroonians who wanted to enter the Civil Service of their territory had to be appointed by the Federal Public Service at Lagos. Complaints were made that Yorubas who were third-class clerks in Lagos came to the Cameroons in more elevated positions. The scare of Ibo domination which resulted in the demand for the separation of the Southern Cameroons from Eastern Nigeria was supplanted in the minds of many, particularly educated, persons by that of Yoruba domination, and when the KNDP was formed in 1955 it used this as a means of attacking the government. Many people felt that the influx of Yorubas into the Civil Service of the Southern Cameroons was due to the fact that the KNC had signed an alliance with the Action Group, a Yoruba-dominated and Yoruba-inspired party.

Regional status was lacking even in nomenclature. Unofficial members of the Legislature were not member Ministers but 'Executive Council members'. Dr Endeley was not a 'Premier' but 'Leader of Government Business'. The official head of the territory's government was a 'Commissioner', not a Governor. There was no 'House of Chiefs'; there were Native Authorities. While critics of Endeley declared that his achievements fell far short of regional status, it is doubtful whether a territory of three-quarters of a million inhabitants could be metamorphosed overnight into a fully equipped region. In 1957 a resolution had been passed in the territory's legislature requesting the implementation of full regional self-government, and when the matter was discussed at another London constitutional conference in 1958, it was agreed. It meant that while ultimate responsibility was still to reside in the Governor-General, since he was responsible for the implementation of the trusteeship agreement on behalf of the British Government, the Commissioner was no longer to be a member of the Executive Council, which had an unofficial majority and was led by a Premier. A bi-cameral system was created for the legislature, with the introduction of a House of Chiefs and the number of elected members in the lower house was increased to twenty-six. For the first time elections were to be based on adult suffrage. At this constitutional conference, it was also agreed that when Nigeria became independent there would be no question of obliging the Cameroons to remain part of an independent Nigeria against her own wishes.

One of the problems which the Endeley government had to face was the obtaining of sufficient revenue to run the government. The greatest single source of revenue was a constitutional grant by which the Federal Government paid to the Southern Cameroons a sum equal to the difference of revenue over expenditure. Federal revenue from the Southern Cameroons included income tax from companies in the Southern Cameroons, such as the CDC, the UAC, Elders and Fyffes Limited, etc., revenue from postal services, import and export dues, excise duties. Money spent by the government in the Southern Cameroons on defence and federal departments was calculated and any difference between the two sums was paid back to the territory. Company tax was the greatest single item of federal revenue and with the limited number of companies in the Southern Cameroons, a bad year resulting in a fall in receipts from company tax could cripple the country's finances. This situation of uncertain revenues did not persist for long since early in December 1955, the Federal Government agreed that if the sum payable to the territory in respect of the constitutional grant plus profits disbursed from the CDC fell below £580,000 the Federal Government would advance the deficit. This analysis should at least explode any myth that Nigeria benefited from Cameroons financial contributions.

Foncha and Endeley

In the mid-fifties there was a constant shuffling and re-shuffling of political alliances and party formations. The most important division came between the two politicians Endeley and Foncha. The initial excuse for this split again had to do with Nigerian politics and occurred when Endeley, forgetting his attitude of 'benevolent neutrality' in Nigerian politics, broke with the NCNC and went into an informal alliance with the opposition group in the Nigerian Government, the Action Group led by Chief Awolowo. However, there were many other reasons for the decision of Foncha and his supporters, most of whom came from the Grasslands, to break away from the KNC and form the Kamerun National Democratic Party. Foncha's declared aim was the secession of the Southern Cameroons from Nigeria with the ultimate aim of unification with the then French Cameroon. Foncha and Jua were supported by the chiefs of Bamenda, Nkambe and Wum who resented the fact that the Grasslands were less economically advanced than the coastal regions. They also resented, in a way, the polished, European sophistication of Endeley and the coastal intellectuals. It is understandable that the chiefs should support the KNDP, particularly as they feared Dr Endeley's plans to reduce their role in regional political life.

John Ngu Foncha was a headmaster of a Roman Catholic school who had been in politics since the early 1940s when he had been an active member of the Cameroon Youth League. Elected to the

John Ngu Foncha

Eastern House of Assembly in 1951, he was an early and enthusiastic supporter of seccession. He left the KNC in March 1955 and formed the KNDP, a party supported by chiefs, university students and those who supported eventual reunification. As a politician Foncha was a realist, who had cleverly swung the enormous influence of the Grasslands traditional rulers onto his side and the side of the KNDP. Many have called him an opportunist and it is true that he often played on people's fears in order to obtain a not entirely unprejudiced backing – for example, in his use of the Yoruba and Ibo scares.

Augustine Ngom Jua

Foncha had the kind of political flair which the politicians of the KNC and KPP lacked. They were too academic for the masses. Endeley had thought that serious political achievements, facts and statistics were sufficient criteria for success at an election, but the elections of 1959 were to prove him wrong. Foncha used the idea of independence and unification to stir up nascent nationalist sentiments and it was with these techniques that he won the election.

At this time, Endeley did not favour either secession or unification. He was content to rest on his laurels and allow the new constitutional changes to have their effect. Despite the fact that he had been at the spearhead of the demands for unification in the late forties and early fifties, it was now clear that he would be content if the territory acquired full regional status within the Federation of Nigeria. In 1957 the KNC and the KPP, both committed to the issue of association with Nigeria, entered into an alliance.

The Ibo question

Ibo immigrants in the Southern Cameroons were an important factor in the separationist movement which was the major subject of politics between 1953 and 1959. Nigeria became synonymous with the Ibos, and 'joining Nigeria' meant 'selling the Cameroons to the Ibos'. In fact it was growing dislike and fear of the Ibos, in many ways encouraged by shrewd politicians, which more than anything else persuaded the people to agree to withdraw from the Nigerian Federations, and the same feeling contributed in no small way to the Trust Territory eventually associating itself with the Cameroon Republic. While the move towards Southern Cameroon separatism from Nigeria and the idea of reunification with eastern Cameroon was always marked by hostility to Ibos, the Bamileke, with their close relations in West Cameroon and their involvement in local Southern Cameroon politics came to symbolise the connection with East Cameroon. However, it should perhaps be pointed out that if the Nigerian connection had become the desired one and the eastern one the undesired one, a similar hostility to the Bamileke, the 'Ibos of the Cameroons', would have been engendered. Even today there is a smouldering hostility to Bamileke farmers who have come down from their Grasslands home and taken over, by dint of hard work and saving, much of the land of the original inhabitants of the forest areas.

In the Eastern Region of Nigeria, the Ibo formed a solid group of well over seven million people, surrounded by three provinces in which other groups predominate: Calabar, Ogoja and the Rivers. Until the second world war or shortly afterwards, their influence in the Cameroons was minimal. After 1945, however, the influx of Ibo immigrants from Nigeria to the plantation areas of Southern Cameroons increased. They came as traders, bringing a certain amount of capital with them. They never became part of the Cameroons scene, however, in the same way as the Bamileke, since they remained somewhat exclusive in the kind of work they did (as petty traders and affluent dealers) and in their behaviour towards Cameroonians. However, since they only began to arrive after the war they had barely had time to assimilate. When the Cameroons was a province of Eastern Nigeria, many Ibos also entered the Civil Service of Southern Cameroons, many of them occupying important posts in government departments, as teachers, tutors, postmasters and clerks, nurses, etc. They also owned innumerable shops, buses, taxis and lorries. They were drivers and mechanics, they owned market stalls and peddled goods in country districts. They worked as farm labourers. The feeling in the Cameroons was that the Ibos made too many sacrifices in order to gain a profit. They were said to feed poorly, trekking over mountain passes and through forests to sell their cloths and petty goods in out-of-the-way markets and under conditions few Cameroonians were prepared to suffer.

Edwin Ardener has written (1960) of the Ibo:

> He has not behaved differently in the Cameroons from elsewhere. He has been his normal self – industrious, cheerful, gregarious, argumentative and with a flair for trade. However, by one of those unfortunate clashes of sentiment that occur occasionally all over the world, these qualities are interpreted by Cameroonians as conceit, brashness, untrustworthiness. The Ibo for his part is no more impressed by the Cameroonian. It must however be faced that the attitude to Nigeria of the villager and illiterate labourer, not excluding a high proportion of literates is coloured, if not determined, by his attitude to the Ibo.

Hatred for the Ibos became an important political fact in the postwar period. In the Southern Cameroons this suspicion of the Ibo was closely associated with anti-Nigerian feeling and was inflamed by rumours, usually ill-founded, about Ibo attitudes to money, to women and to retail trading. It was not surprising therefore that the political parties which advocated separating from Nigeria used the attitudes of the Ibos as a means of fanning the flames of tribal hatred in order to achieve political ends. Although there were other ethnic groups of Nigerian origin in the Cameroons, such as the Yorubas, Efiks and Ibibios, they never caused such widespread and longlasting antagonism with the Cameroonians as did the Ibos. Both groups had used the Ibo scare for their own ends. Ibophobia had been exploited by Endeley and his followers as a justification for the separation of Southern Cameroons from Eastern Nigeria. Later the Ibo scare became the keynote of KNDP propaganda against association with Nigeria and for secession and eventual unification with French Cameroon. Foncha used the Ibo domination scare with great vigour and swung public opinion round in favour of the idea of reunification in this way. It was also used in a general way by Grasslanders against the forest peoples, or in KNDP political struggles with the KUNC. Even the Kom Women's Riot was engendered, in a way, by ungrounded fears that the 'Ibos were coming to take their lands'. Ibos were credited, usually fancifully, with every vice under the sun – bribery, corruption, narcotics, adulterating palm wine and medicines, counterfeiting, stealing, profiteering and seducing local women.

KNC and KNDP

In the 1957 elections, the KNC won a majority and the KNDP

increased its strength from two to five. The elections had been fought by four parties, the KNC, the KPP, the KNDP and the UPC. In 1955 there had occurred the UPC revolt in French Trust Territory (see p. 148) and after its defeat members of the party sought asylum in the Southern Cameroons, settling mainly in Kumba. The UPC gave a deal of stimulus to KNDP leadership and a committee of co-ordination between the two parties had come into existence. It was this which caused Foncha to become an enthusiastic advocate of Cameroon unity. However, the KNDP and UPC did not agree on the speed by which independence and unification should be sought, and the UPC even campaigned against Foncha and the KNDP in the 1957 elections. The UPC's claim for 'immediate unification and independence' received no support in Southern Cameroons and not only were all the candidates defeated but they lost their deposits. It would appear that the country was not then ripe for pressing the unification issue and the fear that the UPC, having failed to achieve its objective in the 1957 elections, might resort to violence as it had done in the East, led to the deportation of its leaders while the UPC and its affiliated groups were declared unlawful societies in the Southern Cameroons. The disappearance of the UPC from the political scene was shortly afterwards followed by the formation of a new party styling itself 'One Kamerun' or the OK Party; the party appears to have been similar in organisation and aims to the banned party.

The differences between the KNDP and the KNC/KPP alliance came out during the two constitutional conferences which preceded the introduction of the 1958 constitution. Both the KNC and the KPP supported the idea of continued association with Nigeria, as a separate region. However, the KNC/KPP delegations at the constitutional conferences declared that they wanted rapid constitutional progress only in order to prepare themselves to take their place in an independent Nigeria. Their reasons for advising continued links with Nigeria included the greater financial and economic benefits available to Southern Cameroons as a region within a Federal Nigeria and the necessity of avoiding contamination with the political chaos of the east. Some individuals decried Endeley's abandonment of unification and one of them, Mr S.T. Muna, even crossed to the KNDP side, along with Galega II, the Fon of Bali. While the KNDP proposed an interim period within Nigeria, they supported the ultimate aim of secession as a prelude to ultimate reunification.

Meanwhile in local politics, the KNC was fast losing support. The Ibo scare was used by many of their opponents to cause people to lose enthusiasm for the Nigerian connection. In Bamenda the Kom

Women's Revolt was bound up with the dispute between the KNDP and KNC. The government, that is the KNC, had undermined its support in the Grasslands by forcing through unpopular contour farming laws, and new education ratings. Several women's organisations, particularly in Kom, had been set up to oppose them and also unseat the KNC. Rumours were also spread that the KNC were selling land to the Ibo, and the incursion of Fulani cattle on the women's land increased anti-KNC discontent. During Endeley's visit to Bamenda thousands of women marched in protest, blocking the road at many points. This kind of agitation was supported by KNDP for political reasons; and Foncha's alliance with traditional and conservative elements continued with reunification. Endeley claimed that Foncha was playing on the prejudices of the electorate; particularly by inciting local people against progressive agricultural measures. He also claimed that the KNDP were telling the people that the government party was selling their land to Nigeria.

At this time the results of the battle between the KNC and the KNDP were not a foregone conclusion. The KNC under Endeley could boast many achievements including the separation of the Southern Cameroons from Eastern Nigeria; the creation of the Cameroons Development Agency and the Marketing Board; an increased revenue; a ministerial system of government; a House of Chiefs; and the establishment of buildings, roads and water supplies. Nevertheless by 1959 the KNDP was beginning to supplant the KNC as the leading political party in the Southern Cameroons. In the elections of the same year Foncha campaigned on his qualified unificationist policy. He won with a bare majority, winning fourteen of the twenty-six elective seats, mainly as a result of the support he had gained in the Grasslands.

The 1959 elections provide a landmark in the annals of the United Republic of Cameroon. The elections were fought on the issue of association of the Southern Cameroons with Nigeria or separation. They brought to power not only a party dedicated to separation from Nigeria, but one which had had the unification of all sectors of German Kamerun as its ultimate, though not necessarily immediate, objective.

It was not, of course, the first time that elections had been contested on these issues. In the 1953 elections the battle was fought over whether the Southern Cameroons should separate from Eastern Nigeria and constitute itself a region or whether it should continue as a province in Eastern Nigeria. Endeley's party had won the election on the question of separation. In 1959 the issue was similar but had assumed a much wider and different import. After Endeley won the 1953 elections he had pressed for the territory to be given the same position as any other Nigerian Region. In this he had been successful and nothing stood in the way of the Southern Cameroons becoming a fully-fledged region. In a speech to the United Nations, after the 1959 elections, he looked back with satisfaction on what he had achieved, and asked what would be the advantages Southern Cameroons could gain by association with a long-estranged French-administered territory. He concluded: 'It will be unwise to abandon a secure and floating vessel which offers us sure landing to allow ourselves to drift in an open life-boat because we hope to be picked up by a new and better vessel which we have not even seen on the horizon'. (Dr E.M.L. Endeley, Address to the UN on 23 February 1959).

CHAPTER 20

Reunification

The United Nations had been under pressure, as the result of political events in Togo and French Cameroon, to find a solution to the question of the status of these two Trust Territories, and the impending (1960) independence of Nigeria meant that the Southern Cameroons now had to decide between the alternatives of remaining in an independent Nigeria or joining an independent Cameroon. Foncha and Endeley left Cameroon after the 1959 elections for New York in order to present their views on the future of the country to the Trusteeship Council and the Fourth Committee of the UN. During the election campaign Foncha had promised secession from the Federation before 1960 if he won.

> Secession from the Federation of Nigeria will place the Southern Cameroons in a position to negotiate terms for reunification with the government of any free section of Kamerun which desires it... The building up of a Cameroons nation once again is a matter which is our concern. The question of reunification is now quite clear; it will be accomplished by independent sections rather than dependent ones under British or French. (*Daily Times*, 8 March, 1955, p. 5).

The KNDP, however, was committed to reunification with an independent Cameroon. Jua, who had resigned from the KNC, was in favour of reunification, and Mukete had made a speech in favour in the House of Representatives in Lagos, in March 1957. S.A. George, another former KNC member, had become converted to the reunification idea and gave vent to his views in a pamphlet entitled 'Kamerun Reunification', written in England. In this he outlined how both the British and French Cameroons could be brought together as one entity. This was probably the first occasion in which concrete proposals were articulately formed on the subject of unification.

It had also become clear that a majority of students who were studying in Nigeria also supported the KNDP plan for unification. Mr Sabum, in an article headlined 'The Case for Secession', had declared:

> The division of Kamerun was an arbitrary and immoral act designed to suit the imperialists. No one can tell me that the division of Kamerun was in the interest of Kamerun. Putting it mildly, I say it was a mistake; a mistake is not corrected by simply accepting it or arguing that it has gone on for a long time. Time does not make a mistake right.

The UPC and independence in French Cameroon

Perhaps the political grouping which most affected Southern Cameroons politics at the time was the Union des Populations du Cameroun. It was founded in 1948 by Felix Moumié, Um Nyobe, Ernest Ouandié and Abel Kingue, and the emphasis was immediately very nationalistic and anti-French, with unification as part of their platform; their motto was 'Unification et indépendance immédiate'. The party had established ties with organisations in the Southern Cameroons such as the Cameroons National Federation and later, the United National Congress. In August 1951 a meeting of the UPC in Douala demanded unification, among other things. On August 22, 1951 the UPC and KUNC held a meeting at Tiko with a view to submitting demands for reunification to the UN visiting mission.

The UPC found most of its support among Bamileke and the Douala peoples, groups which were related to peoples in British Cameroons (the Bangwa and Bakweri respectively) and they used this relationship as well as the factors of trading across the frontiers and labour migration, to support their plan for unification. Um Nyobe had appeared before the United Nations and declared that the division of the Cameroons was an artifical and arbitrary one, benefiting no one but the French and British Governments. The people had common traditions and interest, and according to Nyobe, unification would bring economic benefits. He said that unification was a prerequisite of independence, since otherwise one part of the Cameroons would become independent within the British Commonwealth and the other within the French Union. After Um Nyobe's speech, the influence of the UPC grew and local organisations among the Bamileke and the Douala began to support it in a practical way.

Unfortunately the party began to be blamed for sporadic acts of violence and was also accused of Communist leanings. Harsh measures by the French resulted in further violence in 1955, particularly in Douala. Demonstrators attacked police stations and gaols in Douala and Yaounde and rioting occurred in various parts of the country resulting in twenty-six dead. This violence was put down by police and troops; the UPC was banned and hundreds of its members were arrested. Um Nyobe, Moumié, Kingue and Ouandié fled to the British Cameroons where they were sheltered by pro-unification leaders such as Foncha (see p. 143).

In 1957, however, when the British expelled the UPC from Kumba and a certain division ensued within the group, Moumié, Ouandié and Kingue went to Cairo where they concentrated on setting up a network of newspapers and radio broadcasts and sought support from African leaders. They began to plan organised violence for the Bamileke regions and also the Mungo regions; during the years following violence broke out in east Cameroon and was not entirely quelled till 1970. The UPC in exile provided modern weapons to the rebels in the Bamileke region.

Another group under Reuben Um Nyobe continued to operate in eastern Cameroon. Nyobe is regarded by many today as one of the founders of his country's independence. His activities, as a fearless and elusive outlaw, gave him the aura of hero and he was thought to have mythical and magical powers. Nyobe's base was among the Bassa people; when he found that constitutional means were powerless to achieve his goals of independence and reunification he resorted to increased violence in the Sanaga-Maritime region and also in Bamileke and Mungo areas. There were attacks on the plantations missions and government offices; chiefs, officials and missionaries were killed, kidnapped or wounded. The Cameroon Government in the east under Mbida moved in French troops, armed the local people and conducted large-scale searches in forests and villages for rebel bases. In a period of little more than a year 371 rebels had been killed and 882 arrested. Finally Um Nyobe himself was killed and this strengthened the government's position. In September 1958 a Bassa informer had led a French official patrol to Um Nyobe's hiding place and as the rebel leader tried to escape an African sergeant blew his brains out. When the body was displayed throughout Bassa land the rebels, who had believed their leader could not die, flocked in to lay down their arms. Curiously, the dead leader was later acclaimed as a national hero; he was mourned throughout the country and praised for the part he had played in the nationalist struggle by members of the government who had been his bitterest enemies.

Meanwhile Moumié and his supporters had been consolidating their influence in the Bamileke areas during this period but their opposition to Ahidjo took place mainly at the UN. During a debate in the Fourth Committee, Ahidjo received his most serious challenge from the UPC, who demanded that new elections should be held, because the 1956 elections were held without the participation of the UPC. However, they lost and the General Assembly of the UN resolved on 13 March 1959 that from 1 January 1960 French-speaking Cameroon was no longer to be a Trust Territory and would become instead the independent Republic of Cameroon.

The UPC continued their activities in the republic, although Moumié stated that he would negotiate with Ahidjo only if French troops were withdrawn from Cameroon, an amnesty were granted for political prisoners and elections were supervised by outside observers. When they gained no success, violence once more broke out, with the main offensive occurring in Bamileke areas and those parts of the Mungo inhabited by large numbers of immigrant Bamileke. Guerilla bands operated through the region, sometimes on their own initiative; for a period they held sway in most of the south and the centre of the territory, particularly in the Bamileke region. This was the 'Bamileke revolt', which had its origins in economic factors, unemployment and overcrowding in towns, and dissatisfactions among urban Bamileke. It was also based on the overpopulation in the Bamileke areas themselves and on abuses on the part of the chiefs, as far as land distribution, marriage laws and succession were concerned. Grievances were aggravated by the tendency of the chiefs, many of them French-appointed, to rely on support from the administration rather than on the traditional councils which may have acted as a restraining influence on them. The government crushed the revolt by using French troops, local inhabitants and imposing curfews, roadblocks and special courts to administer summary justice.

Due to political unrest, the independent Cameroon Republic came into existence under President Ahidjo in rather a shaky position. By 1960 the UPC revolt had been contained to the Bamileke region and in the Manenguba region, both of which bordered directly English-speaking Cameroon. A large number of refugees and some terrorists had sought asylum in Southern Cameroons. Nigerian troops had been moved into Southern Cameroons to guard against any spread of terrorism from the border, and, when Nigeria became independent on 1 October 1960, British troops were brought into the territory.

In 1960 Ahidjo was determined to secure his position. He granted a general amnesty for political prisoners and sought to come to terms with opposition leaders. The result of the 1960 elections was that

Ahidjo's party, the Union Camerounaise, obtained a majority. Ahidjo became President and formed a coalition government with members from the larger parties. His position became increasingly secure within the republic and the impact of the exiled UPC became less. Moumié died in 1960, from poisoning in Switzerland, supposedly by an agent of the French Secret Service. After his death the UPC continued to attempt to dislodge Ahidjo and continued its propaganda campaign against the Cameroon Government, but without their leader the rebels had little future. Small bands are still active in the Adamawa mountains and exiled leaders still appear to operate from Cuba.

Early steps towards reunification

In the Southern Cameroons the policy of reunification expounded by the UPC had been received with a certain amount of sympathy from members of the KNDP, at least until the banning of the former party by the Southern Cameroons government. The One Kamerun Party was formed immediately after the departure of the UPC and was believed to be a scion of that party. The founder was Mr Ndeh Ntumazah. The party believed in unification of all sections of the Kamerun but with one major difference from the KNDP. The KNDP believed in a short period of trusteeship during which time the intricacies of unification would be explored before it could be effected. The OK, on the other hand, did not want to prolong independence any longer.

> A conference of all leaders of political thought should be summoned under United Nations guidance to draw up the constitution of United Kamerun. Immediately this is done elections should be conducted under the electoral regulations agreed upon at the Constitutional Conference. These elections may be conducted by the present administration of the Cameroons under British Administration and the Government of the Kamerun Republic should watch all the proceedings. After the elections Parliament should be summoned and independence declared.

The Cameroon Federal Union and reunification

In the early years perhaps the best organised attempt to present a united front on the reunification issue was by the Cameroon Federal Union. In its memorandum to the UN Visiting Mission of 1949 the Union presented its case for unification. It claimed that people near the frontier were obliged to walk many miles to the nearest administrative headquarters to obtain passports in order legally to visit relatives or friends living only a short distance from their own homes;

that certain tribes were split by the frontier and this resulted in the payment of taxes to both British and French collectors; and that petty traders were placed at a disadvantage as they could not move freely among peoples of their own racial stock. The memorandum pointed out that there had been mass immigration to the British zone from the French zone as a result of the partition; and that the situation had given rise to smuggling. It was suggested that immediate steps be taken to facilitate unification – teaching of French and English in schools in the two Trust Territories, establishment of a customs union permitting free trade and the setting up of a joint consultative assembly.

Demands for unification also came from the Balong Native Authority and the Bamenda Improvement Association, while the Bangwa Native Authority asked that the frontier be adjusted so that Bangwa and Dschang might fall under a single administration.

Thus in the Southern Cameroons unification had been under discussion for several years. It was partly involved with the domestic political situation connected with Nigerian constitutional talks, but the influence of the ideas of expatriates from the French Cameroon was important. To a much lesser degree it was also due to a certain amount of sentiment which had an ethnic and linguistic basis, as well as feeling on the part of a vocal minority, particularly businessmen, that frontier regulations were harmful to trade.

In fact, border restrictions constituted a problem. Although anyone entering the British Cameroons from the east needed no travel documents he had to pay customs duties on any goods bought in French Cameroon. On the other hand anyone going into or returning from French Cameroon had to put up with a lot of formalities. British Cameroonians had to arm themselves with a *laissez-passer*, an identity card, and a tax ticket. Small tradesmen and exporters of agricultural produce felt that frontier regulations were too stringent. Border restrictions were increased when the Vichy regime was established in France: individuals with homes on one side of the frontier and fields on the other experienced many inconveniences as did members of tribes whose relatives or chiefs lived on the other side. In the Southern Cameroons many people depended for a livelihood on trading meat and skins, palm oil and palm wine in return for Grassland goods and these restrictions made the exchanges increasingly difficult.

The KUNC and Reunification

Reunification was advocated with the greatest enthusiasm by the Kamerun United National Congress which had been formed in

August 1951 as a breakaway group. In the early years the KUNC established close contact with the UPC and together they sent a petition to the UN General Assembly in July 1952, demanding the removal of all existing obstacles to the free movement of persons and goods across the border dividing the two Cameroons and the creation of a customs union similar to one which had existed between 1916 and 1922. Another organisation of French-speaking Africans, the French Cameroons Welfare Union, also established by Dibonge, put forward early demands for unification. The Cameroons National Federation, which had members from the east as well, had presented a plan for unification at their Kumba conference in 1949. However, when the United Nations Visiting Mission heard the KUNC's request for unification in 1957, the CNF made no mention of unification and emphasised only the need for revising frontier difficulties and establishing a separate regional status for the Trust Territory.

Anti-reunificationists

Dr Endeley was to become a major politician in favour of continued union with Nigeria. Yet even as early as 1948 he had declared himself in favour of the unification of the two Cameroons, and in May 1949 sponsored a conference of political parties from both territories at which he attacked all aspects of British administration, pointing out the more rapid economic and educational advancements made in French Cameroon. They even demanded the transfer of the British Cameroons to French trusteeship. Endeley had also established contacts with UPC and asked for moral support from them on the issue of unification. At this time Endeley was trying to assert the identity of Cameroon and was hoping to remove Southern Cameroons from Eastern Nigeria and bring about political and administrative unity between Northern and Southern Cameroons. He grew discouraged, however, by the lack of interest in the north and their obvious preference to stay in association with the Northern Region of Nigeria. After 1954 when Dr Endeley had achieved the separation of the Southern Cameroons from Eastern Nigeria his energies were directed to achieving constitutional advances so that the territory could achieve full regional status on an equal footing with any other region in the Federation of Nigeria. On 29 May 1958, Dr Endeley stated that although he and his colleagues still believed in unification of the two Cameroons, intervening events and circumstances had removed the question of unification from the realm of urgency.

With the Northern Cameroons absorbed into Northern Nigeria and French Cameroons assimilated into the French Union it now seems unlikely that the Cameroons would ever return to the status it had before 1914. We are convinced that far from being a priority issue, unification should only be achieved by evolutionary means, that is when an independent Nigerian Federation, of which the Southern Cameroons will form a part, would be in an unfettered position to explore the possibilities of union as part of the movement towards the creation of a United States of West Africa.

Again in a speech delivered before the 1959 elections when he was Premier and leader of the KNC, he said:

We had originally dreamt of a united Kamerun which would fuse the sections under British Trusteeship together first, and later incorporate the sector under the French administration. Experience soon taught us how unreal and unhypothetical this dream was... It was necessary to remember the wise philosophy of St. Paul and to realise the folly of persisting in childish thoughts after growing into manhood and my party has hence modified its policy on unification. It is a matter no longer on our priority list.

He was supported by P.M. Kale, leader of the KPP, on the matter of unification, who protested that the way of life of the Southern Cameroons, acquired through association with Nigeria and Great Britain, would be swamped by the influence of four and a half million French-tutored Cameroonians. Another outspoken group in favour of remaining with Nigeria was the KPP under Mbile, who even suggested that those areas which voted for federation with Cameroon at the plebiscite should be permitted to join while the others could remain in Nigeria.

The Mamfe Conference 1959

In 1959 an all-party conference was held in Mamfe before discussions which were to be held at the United Nations, concerning the decision to remain with Nigeria or join Cameroon. The conference was attended by all shades of opinion and the differences seemed irreconcilable. In fact three new parties had been formed in 1959: the North Kamerun Democratic Party in the Northern Cameroons advocating union of the Northern Cameroons with the Southern Cameroons and with the then Cameroon Republic; Kale's Kamerun United Party and Chief Nyenti's Cameroon Commoners' Congress. These last two did not want the Southern Cameroons to unite with the Cameroon Republic. Chief Nyenti's party did not want the Southern Cameroons to integrate with Nigeria but to gain independence as a separate entity. Kale had himself contested the 1959 elections but was defeated.

Any ideas of Southern Cameroons becoming an independent state were quashed by Sir Sydney Phillipson's report to the government at the end of 1959 in which he said that the Trust Territory at its present stage would not survive as a completely independent state and recommended a further period of trusteeship. He considered that this period would give the territory time to develop and test its financial strength. Although actual expansion of the country during the last decade had been considerable and the promise of expansion was excellent, he concluded that as a completely independent state, the Southern Cameroons at its present stage of development would not be viable. A further period of trusteeship of adequate length might afford the Southern Cameroons the time it needed to develop and ·est its financial strength.

In a reply by the Southern Cameroons Government, it was stated that certain of Sir Sydney's conclusions were based on the assumption that the territory would remain separate for a longer time than contemplated and the report's circulation was severely restricted.

Another of the organisations represented at the 1959 Mamfe Conference was the Kamerun Society, a group of educated young Cameroonians who maintained that unification was not necessarily the alternative. Although many people wanted secession from Nigeria they were unwilling for immediate unification since the terms had not yet been worked out. They wanted the question to be 'Do you want to remain with Nigeria?'.

The KNDP wanted the alternatives to be that the Southern Cameroons should remain as an integral part of Nigeria or separate from it and work out its own independence after a further period of trusteeship. Foncha thus maintained that his party did not want reunification to be put as one of the alternatives at a plebiscite. He wanted the Southern Cameroons to enjoy a period of nominal independence before reunification, which was a matter only to be achieved through negotiation between the parties concerned. The KNDP felt that if reunification with the Cameroon Republic was put to the people, the terrorist activities in French-speaking Cameroon would scare the people into voting for integration with Nigeria.

The KNC/KPP alliance wanted the following questions to be put to the electorate: a) Do you want continued association with Nigeria? or b) Do you want to unify with an independent French Cameroon?

On the whole the Mamfe Conference so lacked unanimity that it achieved little; it remained for the United Nations to make the decisions.

The United Nations

At the United Nations it was decided that plebiscites should be held in the Northern and the Southern Cameroons, and that the choice for the voters of the Southern Cameroons should be between joining an independent Nigeria and an independent Cameroon.

A plebiscite had already been held in the Northern Cameroons when the people were asked whether they wished the Northern Cameroons to be part of Northern Nigeria when Nigeria became independent or whether they wanted to decide the future of the Northern Cameroons at a later date. It may seem surprising that it was decided to hold a plebiscite in Northern Cameroons before the Southern Cameroons, but the United Nations had decided that the majority support for union with Northern Nigeria was overwhelming. The results had been a surprise, the Northern Cameroons voting 70,546 to 42,788 to decide their future at a later date. The leader of the NPC, Ahmadu Bello, described the result as a vote against the system of local administration in the Northern Cameroons and not as one against a merger with Northern Nigeria. He also accused British officials, who were easy scapegoats, of subversive activities. In order to rectify these mistakes and as a bait to change the temper of public opinion before the second plebiscite, he made the Northern Cameroons into a separate province in July 1960 and created four new Native Authorities.

The United Nations decided that the questions to be asked at the plebiscite in both the Northern and Southern Cameroons should be: a) Do you wish to achieve independence by joining the Independent Republic of Cameroon? b) Do you wish to achieve independence by joining the Independent Federation of Nigeria? The General Assembly resolved that the administration of the British Cameroons should be separated from Nigeria when the country attained independence on October 1 1960 and that only persons born in the Southern Cameroons should vote in the plebiscite.

The CPNC

Before the plebiscite the British administering authority published a pamphlet which was distributed through the Southern Cameroons, containing proposals of the KNDP and the opposition party concerning the future constitutional and administrative arrangements for joining the Cameroon Republic and Nigeria respectively. The opposition party was now the CPNC (Cameroon Peoples' National Congress). The KNC (the Kamerun National Congress) and the KPP (the Kamerun Peoples' Party), in opposition, following their defeat in the 1959 elections, had a common ideology about the future association of the Southern Cameroons with Nigeria and at a joint convention of the two parties, held at Mamfe on 1 July 1960, plans for a merger were considered and a draft constitution of the new party, to be called the Cameroon People's National Convention, were drawn up with Dr Endeley as President and N.N. Mbile as Vice-President. The CPNC was opposed to unification and claimed that Cameroon could best maintain its territorial identity within the Federation of Nigeria. It also claimed that the Cameroon Republic had not given the same assurances for self-government as Nigeria and maintained that by joining the Cameroon Republic they would lose their House of Chiefs and suffer from a system of land ownership, whereby European settlers were allowed to acquire large properties for plantations. They also foresaw a period of depression due to the poor economic situation in the Cameroon Republic.

The CPNC pointed out that the KNDP which favoured unification with the Cameroon Republic had drawn up proposals with a partner with no experience of federation and a very different political and administrative history. The CPNC had the advantage of knowledge of the Nigerian system and based their proposals on an undertaking which was given to the people of the Southern Cameroons in the event of their joining Nigeria. Southern Cameroons was to become a full self-governing region within the federation with the same powers as other regions. It would have a Governor, a legislature consisting of a House of Assembly, a House of Chiefs, an Executive Council, a High Court with full jurisdiction in civil and criminal matters, and its own separate Public Service.

From the pro-Reunification side came two brief communiqués from the Prime Minister of the Southern Cameroons, Mr Foncha, and the President of the Cameroon Republic, outlining certain constitutional possibilities.

Foncha had formed a government at the beginning of 1960 with himself, M.N. Ndoke, P.M. Kemcha, A.N. Jua, S.T. Muna and J.M. Bokwe as members of the Executive Council.

To fulfil his pledge to the electorate, Foncha, in the House of Assembly on February 11, moved that immediate steps be taken to implement the policy of his government which advocated secession of the Cameroons from the Federation of Nigeria before Independence in 1960. Although the government motion was carried by 14 votes to 12, it should be remembered that in their report to the Trusteeship Council in 1958 the Visiting Mission had held the view that the results of the elections could not be regarded as a decision with regard to the future of the Southern Cameroons, and had suggested the possibility of a plebiscite.

Foncha did not produce any elaborate proposals during his campaign, before the plebiscite. The KNDP was initially upset at the decision to choose between Nigeria and the Cameroon at the 1961 plebiscite, since they did not want to have to face the electorate with a straight choice between the Nigeria they knew and the unknown effects of joining a country with an alien culture and language, and whose political system was so new. Again Foncha brought up the Ibo scare, the possibility of the Southern Cameroons being swamped by the vast population of Nigeria and the old grievances about Nigeria's neglect of the Trust Territory. Foncha, of course, used his prestige as Prime Minister and that of the KNDP as the party in power.

The plebiscite

The plebiscite in both the Northern and Southern Cameroons was held on 11 February 1961, resulting in a vote for union with Nigeria for the former and union with the Cameroon Republic for the latter. The voting was as follows:

	For Nigeria	For Cameroon
Southern Cameroons	97,741	233,571
Northern Cameroons	146,296	97,659

In the south the plebiscite showed that Foncha had the support in most of the divisions; only Nkambe and Kumba voted for integration with Nigeria.

In the north the results of the plebiscite came as a shock to many political leaders in the Cameroon Republic, who had interpreted the 1959 vote for continued trusteeship as an indication of strong support for reunification. All political parties in the National Assembly in the Cameroon Republic consequently voted for a motion to protest to the UNO about irregularities during the plebiscite in the north. Charles Okala, then Foreign Minister, maintained that the results of the plebiscite were falsified and that the people in the north had been prevented from expressing their wishes. The objections included the facts that Great Britain had not separated the administration of the Northern Cameroons from Nigeria as decided by the UNO General Assembly; that the arrival of armed police shortly before the vote intimidated the voters; that the counting of votes and guarding of ballot boxes did not occur under ideal conditions; and that supporters of unification were hindered by discriminatory measures from presenting their case effectively. The Cameroon Republic brought a case against the United Kingdom government at the International Court of Justice at the Hague, but the Court ruled in favour of the British plea that the case was out of order. President Ahidjo consequently declared that June 1 would be a day of national mourning.

In fact there should have been no surprise that Northern Cameroons joined Nigeria. There had never been a strong leader, or a powerful political party, in favour of a merger with French-speaking Cameroon. The people had many things in common with Northern Nigeria, including a language, Hausa. Similarly the fact that most people in Northern Cameroons profess Islam made it easier for them to want to join Northern Nigeria. Before the advent of the British or Germans, Northern Cameroons had been part of the Emirate of Bornu and later when the British administered Adamawa and Benue Provinces as part of this system, they were in fact preserving a *status quo* which the people saw no reason to alter.

CHAPTER 21

The Federal constitution

The Bamenda Conference

Immediately after the plebiscite, Foncha and his advisers began to negotiate for reunification. Most Southern Cameroonians naturally favoured a loose federal structure and proposals for a union along these lines were worked out at the Bamenda Conference held in June 1961. It was attended by party representatives and chiefs who prepared a comprehensive set of proposals as a basis for negotiation with representatives of the Cameroon Republic. It was decided that a clear distinction should be made between the rights of the states and the federation in order to secure the greatest degree of autonomy for each state. Among original demands were those for separate state and federal citizenship, separate governors and a quota of ministerial portfolios at the federal level for each state. There was even a proposal that the capital should be moved from Yaounde to Douala. Southern Cameroonians also wanted a bi-cameral federal legislature; a ceremonial, rather than an executive, head of state; a governor as head of each state, with a prime minister as head of a responsible government; the allocation of a wide range of legislative powers to the states; the maintenance of the West Cameroonian legal system, the retention of the House of Chiefs and safeguards for the continued existence of the customary court system.

The over-optimistic Bamenda proposals were whittled down. Demands for a loose federation and the safeguarding of the powers of the states were irreconcilable with the plans being formulated in Yaounde. In July 1961 leaders of political parties in both the Southern Cameroons and the Cameroon Republic met in Foumban to draw up a constitution for the federation. While Foncha tried to advocate a loose federation, with the Southern Cameroons retaining control of internal affairs, Ahidjo was determined to establish strong central institutions. In fact, the conference passed over in silence most of the proposals of the Bamenda Conference and the Southern Cameroons delegates found it necessary to devote their energies to salvaging a few of their main points. On the whole the basic proposals which reflected South Cameroonian desires to retain certain political prerogatives to the states were ignored or overriden. For example: 'The bi-cameral system in a federation is, without doubt, classic,' said President Ahidjo, 'but it is necessary to lighten as much as possible our parliamentary apparatus in relation to the resources at our disposal' (Press Release, Foumban Conference, 1961). However, while the Foumban conference may be seen as a defeat for many of the constitutional ideals of the English-speaking Cameroonians, several West Cameroon suggestions were incorporated into the final draft of the constitution such as the election of the President and Vice-President by universal adult suffrage, the maintenance of the House of Chiefs and customary courts and the selection of the President and Vice-President from different states.

President Ahidjo in his draft proposals sought to establish a clear preponderance of federal over state institutions, which was in line with his general preference for strong government. It also represented the continuation of the centralised administration which had been embodied in the system of government created by the 1960 constitution of the Cameroon Republic. Ahidjo did not want any diminishment of the authority and power which the UC enjoyed, and in order to retain this kind of control there were proposals for provisions for a wide range of matters which were to come within the federal sphere of competence under the new regime. Thus reunification did not result in a wide degree of decentralisation as KNDP had hoped. One of the reasons was that the government of Southern Cameroons had not received independence before negotiation with the Ahidjo government and hence was in a weak position to demand retention of power by the states.

The constitution of the Federal Republic of Cameroon was fixed in its initial shape at a conference of representatives of the British, the Cameroon and the Southern Cameroons governments, when they met at Yaounde in August 1961, and on October 1 1961, the Federal Republic of Cameroon came into existence.

In the first days of its existence the Republic underwent a series of minor upsets. To many West Cameroonians the constitution was far from perfect. After a while they saw the inevitability of many of the proposals and realised that the constitutional situation of Cameroon is based on historical circumstances. Moreover, it is clearly in the nature of things that a federal constitution can never be perfect. Cameroonians who once extolled the Nigerian constitution, for

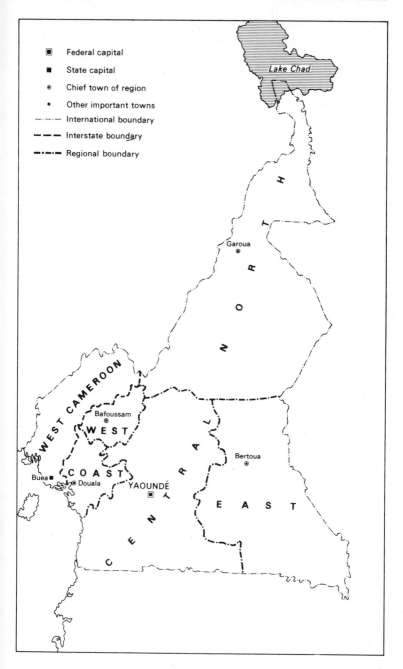

11 Cameroon immediately post re-unification

example, later saw it crumble to smithereens and, as a result, became more than content with their own system: what matters most, they say, is not necessarily the letter, but the spirit of the constitution. In West Cameroon something of a blight was also put on the celebrations, from the British point of view, because most of the expatriate experts and administrators were not asked to stay on after reunification. Nevertheless the Permanent Secretaryship to the Ministry of Finance was still occupied by a British adviser for some time. And Sir Sydney Phillipson was retained for six months. A distinguished West Indian became Attorney-General and occupied this post until 1966. And British advisers remained with the ministries of Education and Local Government.

Some comments on the constitution

In the Federal Republic of the Cameroon there were to be two official languages, while the national flag was the flag of the Cameroon Republic with the addition of two stars symbolising East and West Cameroon. Ahidjo and Foncha became President and Vice-President respectively, with Foncha remaining Prime Minister of West Cameroon. The terms of office of both the President and the Vice-President were fixed, but the duration was indeterminate, a fact which aimed at ensuring stability and avoiding the upheavals which occur when the personnel in political office change over frequently. Although the constitution did not state the powers of the Vice-President, Ahidjo made Foncha responsible for health, mines and power.

The pre-eminence of the President within the federal system was assured by making the state governments dependent on the President. Extensive presidential powers were provided in regard to governmental, judicial and civil service appointments; measures gave the President power to act either exclusively or concurrently with the legislature; the institution of responsible ministry at the federal level was abolished; and the President was given a prime role in the appointment and dismissal of Prime Ministers and governments of states.

By Article 5 of the constitution, a number of subjects were to come under federal jurisdiction immediately on independence, particularly the police and the army. By Article 6 a very comprehensive list of subjects were to become federal matters as time went on. No specific list of subjects was to come under state jurisdiction. Their powers were thus described: 'Any subject not listed in Articles 5 and 6 and whose regulation is not specifically entrusted by this constitution to a federal law shall be of the exclusive jurisdiction of the Federated States, which within these limits may adopt their own Constitutions' (Article 38 (1)). While customary courts and primary education were specifically mentioned as state subjects, other subjects left to the state, by convention rather than constitutional declaration were: Local Government, Social Welfare, Archives and Antiquities, Agriculture, Forestry, Co-operatives, Internal Trade, State public works and others.

President Ahidjo's proposals provided for a constitution more centralised in some ways than even the pre-existing Cameroon Republic. Under the former Republic, Ahidjo had been Head of State, assisted by a Prime Minister who shared his powers with his Council of Ministers, but under the Federation the President was both Head of State and Head of Government. He acquired control over courts, the magistracy and the Civil Service and the right to exercise emergency powers. Due to the troubled political situation of East Cameroon this centralisation was inevitable. The eastern negotiators at the Foumban conference would not easily have permitted greater powers to the West, particularly as the south of West Cameroon, according to the East Cameroon Government, was very similar ethnically and politically to the rebellious south in their own country.

Administrative changes

The most important administrative change in West Cameroon involved the increased influence of the Federal Government. Federal officials supervised the local authorities and district officers assumed a dual role as both district officers and prefects in their respective relationships with the State and Federal Governments. Local authorities were affected when their funds and their tax collection functions were placed under federal rather than under state control in 1965. Many government services are directly subject to supervision of federal ministries – the armed services, the gendarmerie, customs, posts, telecommunications, health, information services and courts. Authority over these departments was put in the hands of an official known as the Federal Inspector of Administration. There were six of these for Cameroon as a whole with West Cameroon as one of them. The Federal Inspector in Buea was responsible for the application of federal laws and for control over federal civil servants. He had wide powers and the support if necessary of the armed forces, gendarmes and police.

In West Cameroon the Federal Inspector became an important personage who wielded great power, controlling operations whose extent was hardly less than that of the State Government. Under the

Federal Inspector came the Prefects, the former district officers who now played a dual role, remaining district officers for state purposes such as local government, but for federal purposes, such as security and the coordination of federal services in the Divisions (or Prefectures) subject to the Federal Inspector. However, local government organs, councils and customary courts based on units set up in the 1930s received constitutional support by the recognition of the West Cameroon House of Chiefs and of the non-federal nature of the customary courts. The inspectorate really had no control over these institutions, as there was a clear boundary between local government, a state subject, and administration, a federal subject.

The gendarmerie
In the period shortly after independence the appearance of the national gendarmerie caused fear in West Cameroon where this quasi-military police force was not part of their tradition. The activities of the Federal Gendarmerie had become notorious. The severities of the new security forces are probably attributable to their low level of education and their experience in terrorist areas in the east. After independence Ahidjo's government feared that the west was going to be a haven for bandits hiding out from the east, and lorries, taxis and buses were continually searched, and travellers questioned about public violence. All this was a disagreeable novelty to the West Cameroonians and complaints poured in. Gradually the eastern gendarmes appreciated the degree of law and order in the West and stopped their displays of authority.

Currency and finance
The CFA (Communauté Financière Africaine) franc became legal tender on 2 April 1962. The banking structure was only slightly changed. Barclays Bank DCO had been long established in West Cameroon and, along with the Bank of West Africa, functioned after independence. In 1965 a branch of the Banque Camerounaise de Développement was established. A new bank with West Cameroon government support (The Cameroon Bank Ltd) opened in Kumba, branches being set up in other towns. Unfortunately the bank met difficulties and in 1966 the civil service salaries could not be paid and financial help was sought from the Federal Government. The Board of Directors was replaced by a committee, mainly of West Cameroon civil servants under the chairmanship of the Financial Secretary.

Economic developments

In 1961, West Cameroon and East Cameroon were two different countries, two different cultures, two different economies. Natural frontiers and independent patterns of communications had kept them apart. Each had a port (Victoria and Douala); roads had been constructed along parallel lines; railways in the east went northwards and not westwards; West Cameroon telecommunications were linked to Nigeria; customs prevented easy commerce across the frontiers. The first changes were small ones: the introduction of the CFA franc as the federation's currency; traffic began to travel on the right; a start was made on the Douala-Kumba rail link; American Aid funds helped to improve the internal road system of West Cameroon: the Kumba-Mamfe route, the Kumba-Victoria route and also the road from Kumba via Tombel to the main Douala-Bafoussam road. The greatest development came in April 1969 with the opening of a new stretch of road which crossed a short bridge over the Mungo river and reduced the journey from Douala to Tiko to less than an hour. Customs barriers had been lifted between the states in 1966 and discriminatory tariffs were abandoned with a resultant shift from the reliance in West Cameroon on British and Commonwealth imports to those from France and the countries of the European Common Market.

Trade was affected through the need to move away from any reliance on Nigeria for manufactured goods and the effect of importing goods through East Cameroon was inflationary. West Cameroon revenue declined through the loss of customs duties on Nigerian goods such as beer and cigarettes. An important export market was lost as Commonwealth preference ceased to operate (in 1966). Nevertheless, there were gains such as French foreign aid and US Aid, which helped to improve roads, communications, education and health services. Industrial growth did not result from unification and Douala and other parts of East Cameroon still dominated. West Cameroon, like North Cameroon, represented only a fraction of the south-east's contribution to the economy and the inevitable conclusion was that for any further benefits to be gained from reunification, a closer integration with East Cameroon was essential.

The plantations

The plantations and the Cameroons Development Corporation were heavily dependent on the Nigerian government for capital after 1947 and also on Britain for export markets. The CDC employed more than half the territory's labour and played an important part in the whole economy. It contributed to the ports and transport systems as well as to revenues through taxes paid to the government. In 1958 bananas contributed almost a third of the total value of Southern Cameroons exports, enjoying a 15% preference over non-Commonwealth imports. The possibility of making up the loss of this preference through trade to the European Economic Community was not very great. Fortunately an arrangement with the United Kingdom meant that the preference was removed only gradually, although in July 1963 it was finally removed, mainly due to West Indian protests, and there was a sharp decline in banana exports and also in other exports.

CHAPTER 22

Post-Reunification politics in Cameroon

Before unification Foncha had negotiated with the British Government for an increase in the number of members in the Southern
Cameroons House of Assembly, from twenty-six to thirty-seven. With
the increased membership divisional representation became as
follows: Wum, Nkambe and Victoria – four members each; Mamfe
five; Kumba seven and Bamenda thirteen. At independence Foncha
and his KNDP enjoyed a narrow majority in the western house over
the CPNC opposition. The provisional arrangements which came
into force after reunification enabled continuity to be maintained
through Foncha's retention of the office of Prime Minister of West
Cameroon while assuming the federal Vice-Presidency. The KNDP's
position was further reinforced by the 1961 elections which gave it
twenty-four of the thirty-seven seats. By agreement between Foncha
and Ahidjo, made in 1962, neither the UC nor the KNDP would be
active in the other's territory. There was a formal alliance between
the parties at the federal level. Three KNDP members were included
in the federal ministry, S.T. Muna as full minister, E.T. Egbe and
N. Ekha-Nghaky as deputy ministers.

On 20 May 1962 following his election as Vice-President of the
Federal Republic of Cameroon, Foncha retained office in the West
but his centre of interest was now Yaounde. This was the height of
Foncha's political pre-eminence in Cameroon politics. The elections
to the Federal National Assembly were held the same month on a
single list system. The KNDP filed ten names and the CPNC ten.
Since the elections were not on single member constituencies the
UC won all the seats in East Cameroon and the KNDP all the seats
in the west. However, the pre-eminence of the KNDP was not to
last long. The basis of Foncha's power and that of his party became
more and more precarious. The factor which caused this and eventually led to the disappearance of separate parties in West Cameroon
was the need to find a successor for Foncha as Prime Minister in the

His Excellency El Hadj Ahmadou Ahidjo

west when his constitutional right to hold both federal and state office ceased in 1965.

In East Cameroon the new President of Cameroon, Ahidjo, was a Muslim of Fulani background, born in Garoua on 24 August 1924. After elementary education he entered the Yaounde school of Higher Administration, a training centre for clerks and technicians where he qualified as a telephone operator in 1942. He was elected to the Assembleé Legislative du Cameroun (ALCAM) in 1946 and was re-elected in 1952 to the Representative Assembly, and again in 1956. In 1953 he took his seat in the Assembly of the French Union in Paris, and was Secretary from 1954 to 1955. He had been President of the Legislative Assembly, Vice-Premier and Minister of the Interior in Mbida's early government.

After the 1956 elections Ahidjo succeeded in bringing about the merger of the various local, traditional and ethnic groups from the north in the Union Camerounaise. When he became Prime Minister in 1958 he was only thirty-four years old. His first step was to construct a government of ministers who were members of the Action Nationale and the Paysans Indépendants as well as his own people. At the declaration of Federation in October 1961, Ahidjo's Union Camerounaise was already the majority party in East Cameroon and its control had been reinforced by the decision of two other parties to join it. Within four years a single party was achieved for East Cameroon. Ahidjo was ready to pursue his goal of a unified national party for the entire federation.

A single party

When the Federal Parliament convened on 27 April 1962, only the UC and the KNDP were represented. In the eastern House of Assembly, despite strong protests from the opposition, the 77 UC members of the Legislative Assembly refused to choose any federal deputies from the opposition and named all forty from the ranks of the UC. A week after the opening of the Federal Assembly Ahidjo and Foncha announced that the deputies of their two parties were to form a single parliamentary group, the Groupe d'Unité Nationale. In elections to the Federal National Assembly held in May, UC candidates in East Cameroon and KNDP candidates in West Cameroon were elected on a single list.

Ahidjo's scheme to integrate the whole party structure in West and East Cameroon was facilitated by the fact that after reunification the West Cameroon party system disintegrated of its own accord and political power came more and more clearly to be focused at the centre.

Foncha's decision to move to Yaounde as Vice-President resulted in a major contest for the Vice-Presidency of the party between Muna, the Federal Minister, and Augustine Jua, the West Cameroon Secretary of State for Finance. Foncha was to remain life President of the party. At the KNDP annual convention, held in Bamenda from 15 August 1963 there was a split in the party over the appointment of the first national Vice-President and the Secretary-General of the party. During the elections it became clear that the KNDP was split into two factions, one which supported Jua and the other which supported Muna. Jua was a foundation member of the party and apart from Foncha he was KNDP's oldest parliamentarian. Foncha, however, supported Muna. He also supported Egbe for the other vacant post, Secretary-General, against Nghaky. But Jua and Nghaky won at the party congress in 1963 by substantial majorities. Jua, as national Vice-President, had a post which by virtue of the KNDP constitution now qualified him to succeed Foncha, the President of the party.

Muna was commonly regarded as a 'federation man', partly because he was bound up in his ministerial responsibilities at Yaounde, although he also saw these as a means of bringing to his state those great constructions and public works which he admired in the east. Jua was held to be West Cameroonian first and foremost and had done good service as Minister of Finance through a difficult economic period.

In March 1965 President Ahidjo and Vice-President Foncha were returned unopposed, which meant that Foncha would now relinquish his post as Prime Minister of West Cameroon. Although it had been understood that Jua, as Vice-President, would succeed him, Muna now claimed that the appointment of the Premier of West Cameroon was the prerogative of the federal President. When KNDP members were consulted in 1965, the vote went in Jua's favour. Accordingly Foncha declined to submit Muna's name to the President and called on him to accept the decision. Muna refused to do so, and he and his supporters were expelled, forming a new party – the Cameroon United Congress, which became the official opposition in the state legislature, when the Presidents of the CPNC and the KNDP coalesced during the same year.

Ahidjo was left to solve the question of who was to be Prime Minister. Despite his personal predilection for Muna he consulted with the KNDP and came out in favour of Jua, a very popular decision at the time. At the same time, however, he quite rightly retained a degree of aloofness from the squabbles in the ranks of the

S.T. Muna

KNDP and retained the allegiance of the CUC party by keeping Muna and Egbe on in the Federal Government.

The KNDP was forced into an alliance with the CPNC by the defection of the Muna faction. This rapprochement between KNDP and the CPNC is perhaps difficult to understand if we consider the history of the two parties during the struggle for reunification in West Cameroon. Nevertheless it was a move which was in harmony with similar moves towards single-party government, which had, as we have seen, been making progress in the east. The *Cameroon Times* of

Tabi Egbe

21 August 1965 carried the following communiqué: 'The leaders of the KNDP and the CPNC parties in West Cameroon, moved by the overriding interest of their people, who along with themselves, have suffered and have continued to suffer as a result of years of profitless political warfare, are alarmed at the fact that a continuation of party political controversy in their young country will only end in the purposeless result of engaging the nation's youthful energies in continued division and strife, while the main problem of the development of our people continues to remain unattended'.

Dr Endeley, the CPNC leader and the state's leading advocate of party unification, became Leader of the House from 1966 onwards. With the Muna faction in close association with Ahidjo and Yaounde, there was already a good deal of support in West Cameroon for national unity. Ahidjo took the initiative by summoning the leaders of the three parties in the West Cameroon legislature to meet with the Prime Minister of East Cameroon and himself at Yaounde in June. He warned them that the problems now facing the Cameroon had caused him to fear the futility of the conflicts engendered by the multi-party system and informed them of his personal conviction that the only solution was the formation of a national party. Within two days he had their agreement to the dissolution of all existing political parties in both states and the creation of the Cameroon National Union (the Union National Camerounaise). By September that year, 1966, the country was to have a national party, the draft constitution of which was drawn up by a twelve-man body – eight UC, two KNDP, one CPNC and one CUC.

The benefits normally associated with a one-party state were well summed up by Gardinier (1963, p. 60):

A multi-party system . . . denied the nation the opportunity to utilise the talents of all its citizens and wasted their energies in interparty battling . . . The continued existence of parties which were above all regionally and ethnically rather than ideologically based made good government more difficult and hindered the growth or national unity . . . At a time, too when Cameroun was beginning to play an important role in attempts at co-operation among French-speaking African states, it seemed imperative that the government should be able to speak and act with the support of the whole nation. With these thoughts in mind UC leaders turned their attention to the best methods for achieving the formation of a single party in which all men of goodwill, regardless of their ideological convictions could work together for the good of the nation.

In an address to the nation on 20 April 1962, President Ahidjo said:

We should understand that the era of many parties and ideological quarrels based on slogans void of all content is over. Ideologies certainly respectable in themselves are apt to end by missing the national ideal, to end up by thwarting the most popular aspirations when they become rabid. It is therefore of urgent necessity that we should rally round one ideal, rally round one programme. I am bent on achieving this end particularly within our assemblies, for whatever some of our fellow countrymen may think, oneness of view on the burning issues of the hour is beyond doubt a vital necessity.

The Cameroon National Union Party

Basically, the smallest unit in the party is the cell which is the key to the life of the party. This comprises thirty to fifty members aged eighteen and over. A quarter in a village or a ward in a town comprises a cell.

A group of cells comprises a branch which is formed from the executives of all the cells which constitute the branch. All the branches within a constituency in an administrative division comprise a sub-section whose executive is elected by the executives of the branches within the sub-section.

Thus a sub-section is co-terminus with a constituency out of which a member was elected to the West Cameroon House of Assembly. A section of the party was co-terminus with an administrative division in West Cameroon and was elected by the executive of the sub-sections within an administrative division. Thus each of the component units of the party, viz: the cell, the branch, the sub-section and the section, has its own executive and the executives of the cells elect the branch executive, the executives of the branches elect the executive of the sub-section and the executives of the sub-sections elect the executive of the section.

In July 1966, a seven-man committee was appointed in each division to organise the cells and branches of the party. This was followed by a four-man team from Yaounde led by the Hon. E.T. Egbe to organise the sub-sections and sections of the party. As a result of the fact that it would take some time to organise the party in West Cameroon, the life of the West Cameroon House of Assembly, which would have been dissolved in 1966, was extended by one year.

In November 1967, the West Cameroon House of Assembly was dissolved and elections were fixed for 31 December, 1967. The electoral regulations included the right to vote. (This applied to persons born in West Cameroon both of whose parents were born in West Cameroon and who were 21 years and over). Every alien woman who had acquired Cameroon nationality by marriage or who had acquired Cameroon nationality by naturalisation and was permanently resident in West Cameroon; and any person of East Cameroon who had been resident in West Cameroon for an uninterrupted period of two years was eligible to vote. The only addition to the 1961 electoral regulations was that of alien women.

The single party system in Cameroon is very much bound up with the state, however. Decisions are made at the centre and communicated to the branches. Politics in Cameroon depends on the predominance of the state over the party. Since the creation of the

UNC, politics in West Cameroon have followed a fairly inevitable pattern. Jua, after his success in 1965, lost ground when it came to the selection of candidates for the single party's list in the 1967 West Cameroon House of Assembly elections. He himself was replaced as Prime Minister in 1968, when the President appointed Muna to that office. Other members of the former Cameroon United Congress gained office as the speaker of the Western House and in the federal government. Later, in 1970, Foncha was dropped as Vice-President and replaced by Muna, who was allowed to continue as Premier in the west, despite the constitutional provision which prohibited this and which had led Foncha to retire in the first place as Prime Minister, thus precipitating the break-up of the KNDP.

At this time, reunification, with all its problems, seemed to most Cameroonians to be a success. Certainly there was no desire for West Cameroonians to return to Nigeria. The suspicion remained, however, that West Cameroon would be swamped, due to the east's greater size and their larger resources; and there was a steady increase in the influence of East Cameroon and its cultural values throughout the country. West Cameroon, in the years after reunification, managed to maintain its separate identity which had neither merged nor been submerged into a single Cameroonian character.

In the political world everything seemed quiet. Economic expansion in the 1970s, at least in the east, was striking, with increased cocoa production and cotton production in the north, development of the Edea aluminium complex and many new industries. In the west there has been expansion in the Cameroons Development Corporation's plantations. There is a general plan aiming to develop areas of backward agriculture. Cameroon now has its own national airline. Abroad it has made its presence felt, taking a strong line on South Africa and keenly supporting the Organisation of African Unity, of which Ahidjo became Chairman in 1970.

Constitutional and administrative changes in Cameroon 1971–1973

Eleven or so years after reunification, a major constitutional change occurred in 1972 with the Federal Republic of Cameroon becoming the United Republic of Cameroon. The first announcement of an impending changeover from a federation to a unitary state came on 9 May 1972 when President Ahidjo informed members of the then Federal National Assembly of the rationale for a unitary constitution in the country.

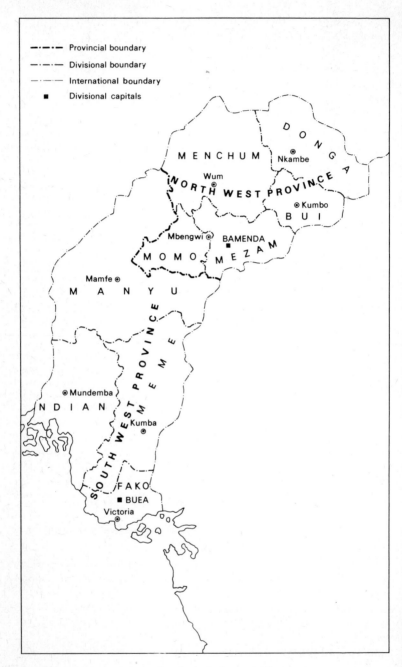

12 The two western provinces after the 1972 changes in Cameroon

a) *The President's address*

According to President Ahidjo, the cumbersome federal structures of the Republic were affecting the development efforts of the Cameroonian people and the functioning of three governments and four assemblies involved considerable expenditure which could have been used in the economic, social and cultural fields. Regarding the budgetary position of West Cameroon the President said:

> It will also be seen that although most services have been federalised the budget of the State of West Cameroon is still experiencing difficulties in spite of a balancing subsidy from the Federation totalling more than 2000 million (francs), that is to say an amount equivalent to approximately three-quarters of the budget. (Cameroon News, 19 May 1972, p. 2)

The change from a federal to a unitary system of government would, according to the President, permeate every facet of the national life. In the field of agriculture which was the mainstay of the national economy, the consequences on agricultural production of an inadequately rationalised and harmonised public policy had to be noted. Similarly, as far as town planning was concerned, the absence of an overall policy of town development directed towards modernisation was making itself felt more and more accutely. The President continued:

> In truth, the federal structures were adopted at the time of Reunification above all to give our fellow citizens of West Cameroon the assurance that the heritage which they were contributing after more than forty years of separation would not only not be ignored but would be taken into consideration within a framework of a bilingual pluricultural state. (Cameroon News, 19 May 1972)

It was evident, however, that it was only at the federation level that bilingualism and pluriculturalism were best expressed, whereas at the level of the federated states no effort was made to introduce them into either public life or primary education.

As a result, the President said . . . : 'now that the federal structures appear to be a handicap to the rapid development of the country . . . it is my profound conviction that the time has come to go further than a federal organisation of the state'.

He said that he would consult the Cameroon people 'who are sovereign and masters of their destiny' with regard to the institution forthwith of a unitary state. Such a transformation would have many advantages. It would lead to a better definition and rational allocation of responsibilities. It would simplify and clarify administrative procedures. It would lead to a more rapid dispatch of public affairs.

It would eliminate duplications, bottlenecks and overlapping within administrative channels and, finally, it would result in substantial savings in consequence of the abolition of numerous administrative structures.

The President assured members of the National Assembly that bilingualism and pluriculturalism must be maintained and developed as they were instruments for dialogue with the world and because 'they are now integral parts of our historical heritage and constitute original traits of our national personality.'

On 20 May 1972 the people of Cameroon were asked to vote 'yes' or 'no' to the following question:

> Do you approve, with a view to consolidating National Unity and accelerating the economic, social and cultural development of the nation the draft constitution submitted to the People of Cameroon by the President of the Federal Republic of Cameroon instituting a Republic, one and indivisible, to be styled the United Republic of Cameroon?

Eighty-five % of the country's 3,326,280 voters went to the polls, and 99.9% voted 'yes' with 176 dissenters.

(b) *Details of the Unitary Constitution*
(i) Fundamental human rights

Both the federal and unitary constitutions affirm their attachment to the fundamental freedoms embodied in the Universal Declaration of Human Rights and the United Nations Charter, but the unitary constitution, unlike its predecessor, spells out what these rights are. Freedom and security are guaranteed to each individual subject to respect for the rights of others and the higher interests of the state.

Everyone has the right to settle in any place and to move about freely subject to statutory provisions concerning public order, security and tranquillity. Both the home and the privacy of correspondence are inviolate. No search may take place except by virtue of the law and no interference regarding correspondence shall be allowed except by virtue of decisions emanating from the judicial authorities.

While the law ensures to everyone a fair hearing, the unitary constitution states that no one shall be subjected to prosecution, arrest or detention except in the cases and according to the manner determined by the law. Furthermore no-one shall be judged or punished except by virtue of a law promulgated and published before the offence is committed. No-one shall be harassed because of his origin or beliefs in religions, philosophical or political matters subject to respect for public order. The freedom of religion and the practice of a religion are guaranteed, and the neutrality and independence of the state in respect of all religions are also guaranteed.

The freedom of expression, the freedom of the press, the freedom of the assembly, the freedom of association and the freedom of trade-unions are guaranteed under conditions fixed by law.

Ownership is the right guaranteed to everyone by the law to use, enjoy and dispose of property. No-one shall be deprived of ownership except for public purposes and subject to the payment of compensation determined by the law. The right of ownership cannot, however, be exercised in violation of public interests or in such a way as to be prejudicial to the security, freedom and existence of property of other persons.

ii) Sovereignty

The unitary constitution has made no changes in the official languages to be spoken, the motto, the flag, the national anthem, the seal and the capital of the United Republic of Cameroon.

National sovereignty is, however, vested in the people of Cameroon who shall exercise it through the President of the Republic and the members of the National Assembly or by referendum.

The existence of political parties is recognised. They may take part in elections and they shall be formed and shall exercise their activities in accordance with the law.

iii) President of the Republic

The President of the Republic is both head of State and head of government. He shall be elected by universal suffrage and must have attained the age of 35 years by the date of election. He shall be elected every five years and may be re-elected. Election shall be by a majority of votes cast.

In the event of a temporary vacancy the President of the Republic may appoint a member of government to exercise his duties but in the event of a vacancy in the Presidency as a result of death or permanent physical incapacity ascertained by the Supreme Court the powers of the President of the Republic shall devolve upon the President of the National Assembly until the election of the new President.

Ministers and vice-ministers are appointed by, are responsible to, and may be dismissed by the President. The office of minister or vice-minister may not be held together with parliamentary office, office as member representing nationally any occupation, or any public post or gainful activity.

The powers of the President are similar to those laid down in the federal constitution.

iv) National Assembly
This will be a 120-member assembly, elected every five years. Laws shall be passed by a simple majority of its members. Bills may be introduced either by the President of the Republic or by any member of the National Assembly.

v) Amendment of the Constitution
Bills to amend the constitution may be introduced either by the President of the Republic or by a member of the National Assembly provided that any bill introduced by a member of the National Assembly shall bear the signature of at least one third of its member-ship, and that an amendment at the initiative of a member of the assembly shall be passed by a majority of its membership.

(c) *Constitutional changes in the Federal Constitution*
The change from a federal to a unitary constitution has in effect meant that certain institutions which were an essential ingredient of a federal constitution have ceased to exist. The federal states of East and West Cameroon no longer exist along with the Houses of Assembly in each of these states and the West Cameroon House of Chiefs. The only legislative assembly in the United Republic of Cameroon is the National Assembly whose membership has been increased from 50 to 120 members and whose members were elected on 18 May 1973.

The post of Vice-President has been abolished and depending on the circumstances stated above the duties of the President could be carried out either by a member of the government or by the President of the National Assembly. The current President of the National Assembly is Mr Solomon Tandeng Muna.

(d) *Administrative changes*
The United Republic of Cameroon is sub-divided, for administrative purposes, into seven provinces headed by governors. In the Federal Republic these were six administrative regions headed by federal inspectors of administration. West Cameroon was both a state with a Prime Minister and an administrative region with a federal inspector of administration.

The governors are appointed by the President and exercise those powers which were the responsibility of the federal inspectors of administration. The governor is responsible for maintaining law and order in his province and is the liaison between the central government and the province.

The federated state of West Cameroon has been sub-divided into two provinces. The division is based on both geographical and ethnic lines. The southern divisions, which are of Bantu region and which inhabit the forest areas (viz Manyu, Meme, Ndian and Fako formerly Mamfe, Kumba, Ndian and Victoria respectively), have been constituted into South-West Province with the capital in Buea. The governor is Mr. Enow Tanjong.

The northern divisions of Momo, Mezam, Bui, Menchum and Donga and Mantung (formerly Gwofon, Bamenda, Nso, Wum and Nkambe) which are of semi-Bantu origin and which inhabit the savannah region of former West Cameroon have been constituted into North-West Province with headquarters in Bamenda. Mr Nseke is both the governor in North-West Province and the senior divisional officer, Bamenda.

Thus with the unitary constitution West Cameroon has ceased to exist as a distinct political entity but since English as an official language has been preserved, the former Anglophone state will be able to preserve its distinct cultural identity. As President Ahidjo said in his broadcast to the nation on the eve of the referendum:

> We know the role that languages play as repositories and vehicles of culture. By affirming our bilingualism in this way, it goes without saying that we intend to offer the cultures linked to our official languages the possibility of developing in such a way as to give birth, in symbiosis with our traditional cultures, to an authentic national culture.

Within a dozen years of independence and reunification Cameroon has undergone an important transformation bringing it more in line with a general pattern to be found throughout the African continent.

Bibliography

Ardener, E., *Coastal Bantu of the Cameroons*, International African Institute, London 1956; 'The Kamerun Idea' in *West Africa*, Nos. 2147, 2148, 1958; 'The Political History of Cameroon' in *The World Today*, xviii London 1962; 'The Nature of the Reunification of Cameroon' in A. Hazelwood (ed.), *African Integration and Disintegration*, London 1967; 'Origins of Modern Sociological Problems Connected with the Plantations System in the Victoria Division of the Southern Cameroons', *W.A.I.S.E.R.*, Annual Conference, Sociology Section, 1953.

Ardener, E., Ardener, S., and Warmington, W.A., *Plantation and Village in The Cameroons*, London 1960.

Ashu, M.N.F., *Pidgin English as a Barrier to the teaching of English Language in West Cameroon*, mimeographed, Welsh College of Advanced Technology, Cardiff 1967.

Bovill, M.E.W., *Caravans of the Old Sahara: an Introduction to the History Of the Old Sahara*, Oxford 1933.

Brain, R., *Bangwa Kinship and Marriage*, Cambridge 1972.

Brain, Robert and Pollock, Adam, *Bangwa Funerary Sculpture*, London 1971.

Burnham, Phillip, *The Gbaya of East Cameroon*, unpublished doctoral thesis, University College of Los Angeles 1973.

Chilver, E.M., 'Native Administration in the West Central Cameroons, 1902–1954' in K. Robinson and F. Madden (eds.), *Essays in Imperial Government presented to Margery Perham*, Oxford 1963; 'Paramountcy and Protection in the Cameroons: The Bali and the Germans. 1889–1913', *Britain and Germany in Africa, Imperial Rivalry and Colonial Rule*, edited by Prosser Gifford and Wm. Roger Louis with the assistance of Allison Smith, New Haven

& London 1967; *Zintgraff's Explorations in Bamenda,* 1889–1892, Buea 1966.

Chilver, E.M. and Kaberry, P., *Traditional Bamenda: Precolonial History and Ethnography of the Bamenda Grassfields,* Government Printer, Buea 1967; 'The Kingdom of Kom in West Cameroon', *West African Kingdoms in the nineteenth century,* edited with an introduction by Darryl Forde and P.M. Kaberry.

Crowder, M., *The Story of Nigeria,* rev. ed., Faber, London and New York 1966.

Diké, K. Onwuka., *Trade and Politics in the Niger Delta, 1830–1885,* London 1956.

Dugast, I., *Inventaire Ethnique du Sud-Cameroun,* IFAN, Yaoundé 1949.

Ezera, K., *Constitutional Developments in Nigeria,* Cambridge 1960.

Fage, J.D., *An Introduction to the History of West Africa,* London 1962.

Gardinier, D., *Cameroon: United Nations Challenge to French Policy,* Institute of Race Relations, London 1963; 'The British in The Cameroons, 1919–1939' in P. Gifford and W.R. Louis (eds.), *Britain and Germany in Africa. Imperial Rivalry and Colonial Rule,* New Haven 1967.

Greenberg, J., *Languages of Africa,* Bloomington, 1963.

Guthrie, Malcolm, 'Contributions from Comparative Bantu Studies to the Prehistory of Africa', in David Dalby, ed., *Language and History in Africa,* 1970.

Hempstone, S., *Africa – Angry Young Giant,* New York 1961.

Johnston, Sir H., *George Grenfell and the Congo,* London 1908.

Kaberry, P.M., *Women of The Grassfields,* HMSO, London 1952; 'Traditional Politics in Nsaw' in *Africa,* xxiv, London 1959.

Kale, P.M., 'Memorandum submitted to the Secretary of State for the Colonies as a member of the Delegation of the National Council of Nigeria and the Cameroons', *Pan Africa,* October – November 1947.

Le Vine, V.T., *The Cameroons from Mandate to Independence,* University of California Press, Los Angeles 1964; 'The Cameroon Federal Republic' in G. Carter (ed.), *Five African States,* Ithaca 1963; 'Cameroon Political Parties' in J.S. Coleman & C. Rosberg, *Political Parties and National Integration in Tropical Africa,* Berkeley 1964.

McCullough, M., Littlewood, M., and Dugast, I., *Peoples of the Central Cameroons,* International African Institute, London 1954.

Migeod, F.W.H., *Through the British Cameroons,* London 1925.

Mveng, E., *Histoire du Cameroun*, Présence Africaine, Paris 1963.

Murdock, G.P., *Africa: Its Peoples and their Culture History*, New York 1959.

Njeuma, M.Z., *Origins of Pan Cameroonism* (mimeo), Accra 1960.

Prescott, J.R.V., *Nigeria's Boundaries. A Colonial Heritage*, Niger 1958.

Ritzenthaler, R.E., 'Anlu, A Women's Uprising in the British Cameroons', *African Studies*, xix.

Rubin, N., *Cameroun: An African Federation*, London 1971.

Rudin, H., *Germans in The Cameroons*, 1884–1919, New Haven 1938.

Ruel, M., 'Banyang Settlements', *Man*, 1960; *Leopards and Leader*, London/New York 1963.

Talbot, P.A., *The Peoples of Southern Nigeria*, London 1926; *In the Shadow of the Bush*, 1912.

Tardits, C., *Les Bamiléké de l'Ouest Cameroun*, Berger-Levrault, Paris 1962.

Van Bleisem, J., *A Geography of West Cameroon*, mimeograph, Buea 1967.

Government Publications
Reports by His/Her Majesty's Government to the
United Nations on the Administration of the
Cameroons, 1947–1959, H.M.S.O. London.

Newspapers
Cameroon Times
Cameroon Champion
Daily Times

Magazines

The Cameroonian
Pan Africa
The Patriot
The Cameroon Voice
The Cameroon Star

United Nations
Reports of United Nations Visiting Missions to the British Cameroons, 1950, 1953, 1956, 1958.

Index

Action Group, 130, 137, 138
Adama, Moddibo, 29–30
Adamawa, 1, 4, 12, 30, 34, 48, 66, 68, 71, 73, 97, 109, 150, 158
Aghem people (i.e. Wum), 46, 48
Ahidjo, President El Hadj Ahmadou, 149–50, 158–60, 162, 167–70, 173, 175, 177, 181
Akwa, King of the Douala, 50–1, 59–60
Ambas Bay, 58, 64
arts and crafts, 13–14, 36–8, 42, 46, 89
Asunganyi, 73
Atangana, Charles, 25, 115–16
Awolowo, Chief, 124, 138
Azikiwe, Nnamdi, 123, 125, 134, 135–6

Babungo, 37, 46
Bafoussam, 43–4, 165
Bafut, 4, 36, 38–40 passim, 46, 48, 67, 68–70, 74
Bagirmi, 12, 18, 33
Bakossi, 4, 25, 38, 55
Bakundu, 4, 25
Bakweri, 3, 4, 8, 25, 50–2, 74, 78, 86–7, 106, 111, 126–7, 147
Bakweri Land Committee, 107, 121–2
Bakweri Union, 128
Baleng, 43–4
Bali, 4, 25–6, 40, 41, 48–9, 66–8, 70, 73–4, 78, 88, 91–2, 109

Bali-Chamba, 25, 27, 34, 38, 46–8 passim
Bali-Nyonga, 37, 48–9
Balong Native Authority, 151
Bamenda (people), 6, 8, 25, 27, 34, 36, 38, 40–1, 46, 48, 78, 138
Bamenda Conference 1961, 159–62
Bamenda Improvement Association, 128, 151
Bamenda (area), Bamenda Plateau, 3, 4, 19, 34, 36–9 passim, 48, 70, 99, 101–3, 109, 111, 120, 129–30, 143, 167, 181
Bamessi, 36, 46
Bamileke, 4, 6, 8, 13, 21, 25, 27, 32, 34, 38, 41, 43–6, 48, 55, 70, 95, 97, 117–18, 141, 147–9
Bamum, 4, 13, 25, 27, 31, 32, 34, 37–9 passim, 41–3, 46, 55, 70, 116
Bamungo, 36
Bandjoun, 44
Bangwa, 3, 8, 38, 45–6, 55, 66, 73–4, 95, 109, 147, 151
Bankim, 39
Bantu, 1, 4, 6–8, 21–5, 27, 50, 181
Banyang (and Anyang), 5, 6, 21, 25, 38, 43, 55, 66, 68, 72–3, 100
Banyo, 4, 39, 47, 70–1, 73, 81
Barombi, 66, 70, 91

Barth, Heinrich, 66
Basel Mission, 49, 65, 74, 76, 77–8, 79, 85
Basho, 72
Basossi, 4, 25, 55
Bassa, 50–1, 74, 148
Batanga, 76
Belgium, 61–2, 81, 95
Bell, King of Douala, 50–1, 59–60, 63
Bello, Ahmadou, 155
Bell Town, 56, 64, 76
Benin, 55, 60
Benue R. and Province, 24, 29, 30, 32, 48, 66, 68, 70–1, 97, 158
Berlin Conference 1884–5, 62–4 *passim*
Beti, 4, 25, 34
Bibundi, 74
Bimbia, 52, 55, 58, 64, 86–7
Bindir, 29, 30
Bismarck, Otto von, 60, 62, 79
Bonaberi, King of Douala, 51–2
Bornu, Kanem-Bornu, 14, 17–18, 27, 29, 32–3, 47, 97, 109, 158
Brazzaville Conference 1944, 116
British, English, 45, 53, 54, 58–62, 64
British Cameroons, 99–112, 118, 123–4, 129, 148, 155; *see also* Northern Cameroons; Southern Cameroons
Buea, 51, 66, 74, 77, 79, 85, 92, 101, 109, 111, 122, 130, 181
Bui (formerly Nso), 181
Bulu, 76–7
Bum, 40, 109
Bushmen, 21–3 *passim*

Calabar, 5, 38, 51, 55, 60, 73, 100–3 *passim*, 141

Cameroon Commoners Congress, 153
Cameroon Federal Union, 150
Cameroon National Union, 173–5
Cameroon Peoples' National Convention (CPNC), 155–6, 167, 170–3
Cameroon Republic, 149, 156–7, 159–60, 163
Cameroons, name of, 53
Cameroons Development Corporation (CDC), 5, 107, 127, 138, 165–6, 175; Workers' Union, 122, 131
Cameroons National Federation (CNF), 130–2, 135, 147, 152
Cameroons Province, 99, 109, 111, 129–30
Cameroons Provincial Council, 128
Cameroons Youth League (CYL) 112, 121–2, 123, 125, 128, 138
Cameroon United Congress (CUC), 170–1
Campo R. and Town, 64, 76, 90
Chad, 1, 16, 95; *see also* Lake Chad
Chari R., 17, 33
chiefs, Fons, 38–40 *passim*, 44, 66, 91–2, 108, 109–11, 114–16, 117, 138
Clifford Constitution, 119
Congo, the, 62, 76, 87, 95
Congo R., 4, 23–4, 50
credit system, 56–7, 63
Creech Jones, Sir Arthur, 125
Cross R., 3, 5–6, 8, 19, 24, 25, 34, 55, 64, 73, 101
currencies and banking, 38, 56, 164, 165

Dan Fodio, Uthman, 29, 32
Diamare plain, 30
Dibamba R., 50
Dibonge, R.J.K., 130–1, 135, 152
Dikwa, 33, 71, 97, 109, 129
divination, 36
Donga (formerly Nkambe), 103,
     181
Douala, 3–5 *passim*, 8, 26, 50–1,
     55–6, 58–66 *passim*, 70, 74–5,
     77–8, 95, 147
Douala Town, 79, 84, 90–2
     passim, 103, 117, 131, 147–8,
     159, 165
Dschang, 44–5, 48, 92, 95, 117,
     151
Dutch, 54, 58

East Cameroon, 117–18, 141,
     148, 165, 169
Eastern Regional Conference, 129
Edea, 90, 117
education, 92–3, 100, 109, 117,
     125, 127, 133, 135
Efik, 4, 6, 51, 142
Egbe, E.T., 167, 170–2, 174
Elat, 77
Endeley, Chief, 111
Endeley, Dr Emmanuel, 121–2,
     123, 129, 131–2, 134–8, 140,
     142–6, 152, 156, 173
Endeli, Chief, 74
epidemics and diseases, 88–9, 117
Ethiopea, 13
Eye Njie, 51

Fako (formerly Victoria), 1, 5, 6,
     25, 26, 181
Fali, 30, 32, 37
Fang, 4, 25, 27, 34, 50, 74
Federal Republic of Cameroon,
     Constitution of, 159–63

Fernando Po, 3, 26, 53, 55, 58
Fezzan, 12, 14–16
Fon, *see* chiefs
Foncha, John Ngu, 122, 131, 133,
     138–40, 142–4, 146, 148, 154,
     156–7, 159, 162, 167, 169–70,
     175
Fontem, 36, 38, 70, 73
Fonyonga, Chief, 73
Foumban, 34, 41–2, 46, 88, 117;
     Conference, 159–60, 163
French, 42, 45, 54, 59–61 *passim*,
     64, 71, 95, 147
French Cameroon, 97, 101, 104,
     113–18, 129, 138, 146, 147–9
French Cameroons Welfare
     Union (FCWU), 120, 131, 152
French colonial policy, 113–16
Fulani, 4, 12, 21–2, 26–32, 34,
     71, 108–9, 144, 169; raids and
     jihad, 3, 16, 18, 27, 29, 41, 43,
     47, 48, 55
Fungom, 46, 48

Gabon, 1–3, 22–3, 27, 50, 76, 77,
     95
Galega I, 67–8
Galega II, Fon of Bali, 123, 143
Garamantes oasis, 14–15
Garoua, 29, 31, 71, 73, 169
Gbaya, 30, 32
George, S.A., 132–3, 136, 146
George Town, 56
German Colonial Society
     (Deutsche Kolonialgesellschaft),
     70, 80–1
German-Douala Treaties, 62–4,
     77
German Kamerun Protectorate,
     end of, 95
German Kamerun Treaty, 70
Germans, 5, 31, 42, 43, 45, 60–

71, 104; brutality of, 93;
colonial administration of, 26,
56, 90–4; explorations of, 65–
71

Gesellschaft Nordwest-Kamerun,
81

Gesellschaft Süd-Kamerun, 81,
85

Ghana, 14, 17, 54

Gladstone, William E., 59

Grassfields, Grasslands, 1, 4, 19,
34, 40–1, 43, 46–8 *passim*, 68, 70,
73–4, 88, 95, 103, 138–9, 144;
Eastern, 13, 36, 42, 49

Gravenreuth, 74

Groupe d'Unité Nationale, 169

Guider Region, 30

Gwofon (now Momo), 181

Haman Dandi, 30

Hanno the Carthaginian, 9–11,
14, 50

Hausa, 4, 21, 26, 29, 31–2, 40,
71, 81, 87, 158

Henry the Navigator, Prince, 11

Herodotus, 14

Hewett, Edward, 60–1, 62

Hickory Town, 56, 64, 76

Ibadan Conference, 129–30

Ibibios, 142

Ibos, 135, 137, 139, 141–2,
143–4, 157

indirect rule, 71, 91, 100, 107–8,
109, 118, 124

Islam, 12, 14, 16, 27–30, 32, 42,
70, 78, 158

Isuwu, 51–2, 86–7

ivory, *see* trade goods

Jamot, Dr Eugene, 117

Jantzen und Thormählen, 63, 79,
86

Jua, A.N., 138, 146, 156, 170, 175

judicial systems, 91, 111, 116,
126, 136

Jukun, 40

Kale, Peter M., 121–2, 123, 125,
135, 153; Kale Memorandum,
125–7

Kamerun National Congress
(KNC), 135–6, 139–40, 146,
153, 155

Kamerun National Democratic
Party (KNDP), 137–9, 142–4,
146–7, 154–7, 160, 167,
169–72, 175

Kamerun People's Party (KPP),
135–6, 140, 143, 153, 155

Kamerun Society, 154

Kamerun United National
Congress (KUNC), 121, 130,
132–3, 147, 151–2

Kamerun United Party, 153

Kangsen, Rev. J., 132, 136

Kapsiki, 3, 4, 21, 29

Katsina Ala R., 34, 46

Keyaka-Ekoi, 5, 8, 24, 25, 72, 100

Kimi, 39, 47

kingship, 41–2; divine, 13–14, 40

Kingue, Abel, 147–8

Kirdi, 27, 29, 101

Koko, 50–1, 74

Knorr, Admiral, 77

Kom, 36, 38, 39–40, 46, 48, 109

Kom Women's Riot, 142, 144

Kotoko kingdoms, 13, 18, 32, 66

Kovifem, 39

Kribi, 79, 81, 87, 90

Kumba (now Meme), 4, 36, 39,
40, 91, 101, 106, 109, 126, 129,
132, 134, 143, 152, 157, 165,
167; Conference 1949, 152

kumi, 56, 63
Kumze, 45
Kuva Likenye, Chief, 74

labour, 68, 70, 72–4 *passim*, 86–9,
    106; forced, 98, 104, 117, 118
Lake Chad, 1, 4, 12, 17, 21, 33
lamidats, lamidos, 22, 29–32, 71
land, 44, 75, 84–6, 98, 106–7,
    125–6
languages, 19–26, 92, 121, 162,
    181
League of Nations, 53, 95, 98–9,
    107, 119, 120
Leighton Wilson, Rev J., 76
Leist, 90, 94
Lekele R., 4
Logone Birni, 18, 66
Logone R., 30
Lugard, Lord, 107
Lyttelton Constitution, 135–8

Macaulay, Herbert, 119, 123
MacDonald, Sir Clavel, 64
Macpherson Constitution,
    128–34, 135
Mali, 14, 17
Mamfe, 72–3, 101, 106, 109, 122,
    128, 131, 134, 135, 156, 165,
    167
Mamfe conferences, 128, 135,
    153–4
Mamfe Cross River Section, 3
Mamfe Improvement Union, 128
Manenguba, 3, 149
Manga Bell, King, 75
Manga Williams, Chief, 107,
    109–11, 123, 125, 128, 132
Mankon, 36, 47, 48, 68, 74
Manyu (formerly Mamfe), 5, 6,
    25, 47, 70, 72, 103, 181
Margi, 4, 21

Marienberg, 77
Maroua, 19, 30–1, 71
masks, masked societies, 26, 41
Massa, 17–18, 29
matrilineal institutions, 36, 46, 48
Mbam R., 30, 39, 41, 46
Mbaw, 4, 34, 39
Mbembe, 5, 40, 46–7
Mbile, N.N., 130–2, 135–6, 153,
    156
Mbo, 4–6 *passim*, 8, 25, 38, 44, 97
Mboko, 51, 52, 86
Mbonge, 70
Mbouda, 44
Mbum, 30, 34, 47, 48
Meme (formerly Kumba), 6, 25,
    66, 91, 181
Menchum (formerly Wum), 181
Mezam (formerly Bamenda), 39,
    181
missionaries, mission stations, 26,
    49, 52, 58–9, 61, 64, 65, 72,
    76–8, 90–2 *passim*, 107, 109,
    126–7; Baptists, 76, 77;
    Catholics, 77, 79; Lutherans,
    76; Presbyterians, 76–7; *see also*
    Basel Mission
Mofu, 29
Mogamo, 47
Momo (formerly Gwofon), 181
Moumié, Felix, 147–8, 149–50
Mount Cameroon, 1, 3, 5, 9, 11,
    50, 51, 58, 66, 74, 86
'Mpawmanku wars', 72
Mukete, Chief, 129, 146
Muna, S.T., 132–3, 134–6, 143,
    156, 167, 170–1, 173, 175
Mundame, 66, 70, 91
Mundani, 38, 47
Mungaka, 25, 26, 49, 78
Mungo R., 44, 55, 66, 148–9, 165
'Munshi', 46, 47, 73

Nachtigal, Dr Gustav, 60–1, 62–3, 66, 77, 79

National Council of Nigeria and the Cameroons (NCNC), 122–3, 124, 127, 130, 132–5, 138

National Democratic Party, 119

nationalism, 109, 111, 120, 122–3, 130, 140

Native Authorities, 109–11, 114, 124, 126, 134, 137, 155

Ndian, 25, 181

Ndobo, 39, 46

Ndop plain, 4, 34, 39, 46

Ngaoundere, 30–1, 71

Nguti, 66

Nigeria, 1–3, 4–6 passim, 12, 14, 21, 25–6, 27, 29, 32, 66, 73, 95–6, 99, 165; and British Cameroons, 100–1, 104, 109, 111, 119, 121–5 passim, 128–46 passim, 149, 152–3, 155–8; Eastern Regional Crisis 1953, 134–5

Niger R., 1, 12, 21, 32, 66

Njoya, King of Bamum, 42–3, 75, 116

Nkambe (now Donga), 103, 138, 157, 167, 181

Nkongsamba, 91, 117

Nok culture, 12–14

Northern Cameroons, 99–100, 103, 108, 121, 129, 135, 152–5, 157–8; administration of, 109–11

North Kamerun Democratic Party, 153

Noun R., 41, 43

Nsaw, 4, 13, 32, 36, 38, 39–40, 41, 47, 109

Nso (now Bui), 181

Nsei, 36

Ntumazah, Ndeh, 150

Nyenti, Chief, 153

Nyong R., 76

Oban-Rumpi range, 3, 4

Oil Rivers Protectorate, 62

Okala, Charles, 121, 157

'One Kamerun' (OK) Party, 143, 150

Ossidinge, 73

Ouandié, Ernest, 147–8

Pallotin Fathers, 77

Pana Mountains, 30

Partie Socialiste Camerounaise, 121

patrilineal institutions, 36, 46

Pavel, 70, 73

Pidgin English, 5, 26

plantations, plantation crops, 5, 75, 78–9, 83–5, 86, 88, 93, 101, 103–4, 106, 107, 117, 156, 165, 175

polygyny, 32, 41

Portuguese, 50, 53–4, 58, 61

Proto-Bantu, 24, 25

Pückler-Limburg, Graf von, 72–3

Puttkamer, Governor, 71, 85, 90, 94

Pygmies, 21–3

Rabeh, 33, 71

railways, 91, 93, 95, 117–18, 165

Richards Constitution, 123–4, 125, 127, 128

Rio del Rey, 4, 5, 55, 58, 64, 90–1

roads, 93, 101–3, 117–18, 165

Romans, 14

Saker, Alfred, 26, 52, 58

Sanaga R., 25, 77, 148

Sao culture, 12–13, 14, 17–18, 27
Sao Thomé, 3, 54, 83
secret societies, 36–8 *passim*, 40–1
Semi-Bantu, 6, 21, 25–6, 27, 35, 181
Senegal, 21, 28, 54, 87
Shuwa Arabs, 32
slaves, slave trade, 15–16, 18, 27, 30–1, 38, 47, 48, 51, 54–6, 58–9, 70, 87, 98, 108
Soden, Governor, 85, 90
Sokoto, 29, 31
Southern Cameroons, 99–104, 118–121 *passim*, 126, 128, 129, 135–8, 141–7, 149–60; administration of, 109–11
Sudan, 1, 12–13, 14, 21, 27–8, 33, 53

Tadkon, 47
Takum, 34, 68
Tanjong, Enow, 181
taxes, taxation, 73, 75, 88, 91–2, 109, 151
Tibati, 39, 70–1
Tikar, 4, 25, 27, 32, 34, 37, 38–40, 48
Tiko, 3, 5, 90, 104, 147, 165
Tingilin, 30
Ti smiths, 37
Tiv, 24–5
Tombel, 4, 165
trade, 14–15, 32, 38, 51–2, 53–8, 60–1, 70–2, 78, 81, 90, 103, 165
trade goods, 32, 51, 54–5, 68, 70–2, 81, 83
trading monopolies, 65, 74–5, 77, 79, 81
tribal organisation, 40–1, 44, 47–8, 89

Um Nyobe, Reuben, 121, 147–8

unification, reunification, 100, 121, 138, 140, 143–4, 146–8, 150–4, 156, 159, 162, 165, 171, 175
Union Camerounaise (UC), 150, 160, 167, 169
Union des Populations du Cameroun (UPC), 45, 121, 129, 130, 143, 147–50, 152
United Nations, 145–6, 149, 152; charter, 120; missions, 93, 100, 120–1, 130, 147, 150, 152, 156; plebiscites, 100, 121, 155, 157; trusteeship, 53, 107, 112, 120–1
United Republic of Cameroon, 144, 175–81

Victoria (now Fako), 106, 109, 126, 131, 132, 167, 181
Victoria (town), 52, 58, 64, 65, 76, 79, 90, 92, 101, 104, 165
Vieter, Bishop, 77

Westafrikanische Pflanzungsgesell-schaft, Victoria (WAPV), 85, 104
West Cameroon, 99, 141, 160, 163–5, 167, 169, 171–5, 177, 181
Widekum, 8, 34, 40, 46–8
William, King (Chief Bile), 52, 111
Woermann, Adolf, 56, 60, 62–3, 77, 79–80, 86, 90
World War I, 95
World War II, 120, 122
Wouri R., 5, 50–1, 53, 66
writing system, 42–3
Wum (now Menchum), 46, 138, 167, 181
Wute, 25, 32, 34, 48

Yaounde, 19, 42, 70, 74, 79, 81,

88, 90–2 *passim*, 95, 115–16, 117, 148, 159, 167–70 *passim*, 173, 174
Yoko, 22, 70

Yola, 30, 31, 64, 71, 92, 97, 109
Yorubas, 137, 139, 142

Zintgraff, 48–9, 66–70, 72, 91